HIP HOP

Hip Hop

Also by this author:

Hip Hop
Art After Midnight
Adventures in the Couterculture
Octopus Conspiracy
True Ghost Stories
Cannabis Cures Cancer?
My Tragic Love Affair
Paradigms and Perceptions
My Chomsky Critique
The Bitcoin Revolution
Dirty Money, Secret Societies and Killing JFK
Magic, Religion and Cannabis
1966
Killing Lincoln: The Real Story

Copyright 2014 Steven Hager, all rights reserved.
ISBN 978-1503281585

For the first generation

Kool Herc, circa 1976. The seldom photographed Sa-sa, perhaps the greatest of the original break dancers (and inventor of the "Sa-sa drop) is partially seen on the left; photo courtesy Coke La Rock.

Introduction

Located near the intersection of the Cross Bronx and Bronx River expressways, the Bronx River Project looks like a lot of other massive, low-income housing projects in New York City: a circle of unadorned, 15-story brick buildings circling two small playgrounds. Unlike the nearby South Bronx located due west of here, this project and its surrounding neighborhood survived the last few decades relatively intact, with few buildings gutted and abandoned. In fact, the surrounding community appears calm and peaceful and is filled with row and row of identical two-story brick houses, most of which have tiny concrete yards framed by cast-iron fences.

On February 2, 1982, Afrika Bambaataa held his third annual party celebrating Black History Month at Bronx River Community Center, a squat, fortress-like structure in the center of the project. Around noon, a sound system was installed in the center's gymnasium, and a few hours later dance music began blasting out of a pair of 5-foot speaker columns. Almost immediately, a smattering of young black males began drifting into the gym. Most of them lounged against the back wall and stared vacantly at the stage.

It would be difficult to designate a precise moment when the concert officially began. It's fairly easy, however, to pinpoint the moment it first stopped: at 7:15 pm, shortly after a gunfight broke out just outside the center's main entrance. The shots sounded surprisingly innocuous—"like a string of firecrackers," someone later said—and most of the audience never heard them because they were dancing to *I Want You Back* by the Jackson Five. It didn't take long, however, for news of the fight to reach every corner of the gym, and the crowd grew restless and uneasy.

No one knew exactly what had happened, but a lot of wild rumors were spreading. Everyone's worst fears seemed confirmed when a housing cop, the sole representative of adult authority, reached behind a stack of records, retrieved an automatic rifle, and ran out the back door. The music stopped and the overhead lights came on. Squinting from the sudden brightness, the audience drifted aimlessly around the room. "Yo, man, what's goin' on outside?" someone asked.

The barrel-chested Bambaataa stood stoically behind the turntables, a set of earphones turned askew on his head, the expression on his face changing from concern to anger to disappointment. He noticed a group edging aggressively toward the main entrance and picked up the microphone. "Where you goin'?" he asked, his authoritative voice booming over the sound system. "There ain't nothin' goin' on out there." He paused and then addressed the whole audience. "No violence...no violence...no violence," he said evenly, his voice having a pronounced effect on the more skittish ones in the group. He set the needle on a James Brown record and let it play a few seconds before abruptly lifting it. A few members of the audience—the hard-core dancers—moaned. "You like that?" taunted Bambaataa. "Music. That's what I'm talkin' about." He put the needle back on the record and let it play. The lights went out and the crowd began to dance.

An hour later, the moment of panic had been forgotten and the gym was filled with several hundred happy, sweating, undulating bodies. The temperature inside the gym had to be close to 90 degrees, yet few people removed their coats. The stage, already jammed with equipment, had also become crammed with people, some of whom were waiting to perform, most of whom were just trying to get as close to the action as possible.

Bambaataa periodically ordered the stage cleared, in which case his security forces halfheartedly ushered a few people off the stage. "You can come back later, but you have to get off now," they told the unfortunate few while ejecting them. Finally, Chief-rocker Busy Bee Starsky, the rap equivalent of a lead-off batter, grabbed the microphone and pranced across the stage, cutting a wide swath through the crowd. The dancers, most of whom were dressed in hooded sweatshirts, leather bomber jackets, basketball shoes, and jeans, pressed closer to the stage.

"Everybody who likes sex, throw your hands in the air!" screamed Busy Bee. The audience threw up its hands and roared in approval. Busy Bee was clearly a favorite here.

"What's the name of this nation?" he shouted, his wiry body quivering with energy.

"Zulu! Zulu!" chanted the audience.

"And who's gonna get on down?" asked Bee with a smile.

"Bambaataa! Bambaataa!"

For the next six hours a succession of rappers vied for control of the microphone. Some came in groups of four or five, others performed solo. Guest deejays replaced Bambaataa at the turntables, manipulating, distorting, and repeating segments of records until the original songs were barely recognizable. Young dancers paraded to the stage, flipped in the air, and spun on their backs, their shoulders, their heads. This was my first glimpse of a hip hop performance in the Bronx and I was the only white guy in the gym.

I couldn't help but marvel at the immense creativity these kids displayed and it reminded me of my own youth in the 1960s, when my generation took up musical instruments and created garage rock and psychedelic art. In fact, immense cultural shifts probably usually emanate from the youth who have not yet been indoctrinated or inducted into adult ceremonial rituals. When 15-year-olds start manifesting immensely creative ceremonies, rest assured that energy is as clean and uncontaminated as spirituality gets. It would take time for me to fully comprehend the nature and origins of all these energies manifesting before me, but I already knew this search was going to take me off on another great adventure.

Chapter 1: The Bronx on Fire

In 1955, it seemed like everyone wanted to live in the Bronx. Second-generation immigrants from Manhattan's impoverished Lower East Side, blacks leaving the South, Puerto Ricans fresh from La Guardia airport, servicemen returning from overseas duty—they poured across the Harlem River in search of the American Dream, which would be lived out in an art deco apartment building overlooking the Grand Concourse, New York's finest boulevard and the Bronx equivalent of the Champs Elysees.

"The Bronx at that time was a paradise compared to [Harlem]," recalled Victor George Mair, who soon joined the migration northward. "Everything was so neat, so clean, so tidy, so orderly. I mean they were living in luxury."

Queens was dubbed "the borough of private houses," while the Bronx was known as "the borough of apartment buildings." Despite all the buildings, it wasn't easy to find a place to live. Rent controls enacted during World War II had kept the housing market tight and leases were usually kept in the family, handed down like priceless heirlooms. Most buildings, especially those on the Concourse, had long waiting lists.

It seemed impossible that within a few years this distinguished, orderly neighborhood could begin to suffer a precipitous decline that would not be slowed until more than 1,500 buildings were left abandoned. Life-long Bronxites moved out in droves, entire neighborhoods were decimated by arson, and the once beautiful landscape of the South Bronx became so dominated by rubble-strewn lots that some visitors said it reminded them of Dresden after the war.

"It happened so slowly and to such an extent that I wasn't even aware of change until one day I decided to take a walk around the block and discovered we had no block," Mair told a historian from the Bronx Museum of the Arts. "Then I decided to take a walk around the neighborhood and found that we had no neighborhood."

The beginning of the end came in 1959, when Parks Commissioner Robert Moses began building an expressway through the heart of the Bronx. It was apparent that Moses cared little for the small, tight-knit communities that stood in his way. "When you operate in an overbuilt metropolis, you have to hack your way through with a meat ax," said Moses.

Marshall Berman vividly recalled the effects of Moses' ax in his book *All That Is Solid Melts Into Air*. "My friends and I would stand on the parapet of the Grand Concourse, where 174th Street had been, and survey the work's progress—the immense steam shovels and bulldozers and timber and steel beams, the hundreds of workers in the variously colored hard hats, the giant cranes reaching far above the Bronx's tallest roofs, the dynamite blasts and tremors, the wild, jagged crags of rock newly torn, the vistas of devastation stretching for miles to the east and west as far as the eye could see—and marvel to see our ordinary nice neighborhood transformed into sublime, spectacular ruins."

The middle-class Italian, German, Irish, and Jewish neighborhoods disappeared overnight. Impoverished black and Hispanic families, who dominated the southern end of the borough, drifted north. Businesses and factories relocated. The open-air market on Bathgate Avenue was destroyed.

Along with the poor came their perennial problems: crime, drug addiction, unemployment. They also brought a smoldering sense of injustice, which exploded in nearby Harlem with a wave of "race riots" in 1965. Although there were no riots in the Bronx, it wasn't long before a Black Panther Information Center opened on Boston Road.

In 1968, Robert Moses completed his second grand project for the Bronx, a 15,382-unit co-op apartment complex, located on the northern edge of the borough and conveniently serviced by one of his expressways. Vacating their comfortable apartments, the Bronx middle class poured into Co-op City so fast one might have thought the hounds of hell were chasing them. With vacancy rates skyrocketing, reputable landlords panicked and quickly sold out to professional slumlords, who began buying, selling and trading buildings at a furious rate.

In the 1950s, gang jackets had been the embroidered satin variety favored by high school letterman, but in the 1960s, almost all colors became based off the jean vests pioneered by the Hell's Angels, who had achieved notoriety from their connection with the counterculture in San Francisco.

Coincidentally, 1968 marked another important development in the Bronx's history. During that summer a group of seven teenage boys began terrorizing the vicinity around the Bronxdale Project on Bruckner Boulevard in the Southeast Bronx. In itself, this might not seem significant, but it was the presence of this group that laid the groundwork for a surge of street gang activity that overwhelmed the Bronx for the next six years.

At first, the group called itself the Savage Seven and they were known primarily for beating up bus drivers and generally wreaking havoc around the Bronxdale Community Center. However, it wasn't long before other boys wanted to hang out with the Seven. The ranks swelled to several dozen and the name had to be changed. They chose "The Black Spades," which worked out nicely because they could take the spade emblem from a deck of cards, sew it on the back of a jean jacket, and wear colors, just like the Hell's Angels. It wasn't long before a spray-painted Black Spade emblem began to appear in every hallway in the Bronxdale Project.

Gary Weiss produced two documentaries on New York City streetgangs in the 1970s, and even shot inside the Savage Skulls clubhouse. Weiss credits Benjamin "Yellow Benjy" Melendez for sparking the resurgence of streetgangs in 1967 when he founded The Ghetto Brothers. The Savage Skulls were headed by Filipe "Blackie" Mercado. Several gangs joined the Skulls in an epic battle against the Fort Apache police after a member of the Skulls was beaten in the street by a cop.

The Black Spades may have started out as kids aged twelve to fifteen, but collectively they assumed a power far beyond their age, a power that struck instant fear in the hearts of their elders. You couldn't pick a fight with one Spade without picking a fight with all of them. Together, they were invincible. They could swagger into any project in the Bronx and bully anybody.

The boys who lived in the Castle Hill Project in the North Bronx always hated the boys in the Bronxdale Project. It was one of those feuds that started shortly after the projects were built and never went away. Realizing it was time to get organized, the Castle Hill Project created a group called "Power," whose primary activity was to get into fights with member of the Black Spades. Wanting to do the Spades one better, they began creating divisions of Power in other projects.

Almost overnight, street gangs appeared on every corner of the Bronx. Realizing they had a significant problem on their hands, the New York Police Department created the Bronx Youth Gang Task Force, a 92-member squad commanded by Deputy Inspector William Lakeman, who spent his first year on the job compiling dossiers on suspected gang leaders. By 1970, estimates of gang membership ran as high as 11,000. Reported assaults in the Bronx had risen from 998 in 1960 to 4,256 in 1969. Burglaries during the same period had increased from 1,765 to 29,276.

It wasn't long before the media became interested in the street gangs, and, strangely enough, most of the early articles were somewhat positive, focusing on the gangs' attempts to wipe out heroin addiction in their neighborhoods. Howard Blum wrote in the *Amsterdam News*:

There are no junkies on Hoe Avenue in the South Bronx. The Royal Charmers ordered all junkies and dealers to leave their turf. Most left quickly. Those who stayed were beaten or killed. The Royal Charmers were brutal, but effective: there are no junkies on their turf.

On an August afternoon last summer a bedsheet was tied to two corner lampposts and stretched high across 173rd Street and Hoe Avenue in the Bronx like a campaign banner. The message on the sheet, written in large, childlike black letters, was direct: 'No junkies allowed after 10 o'clock. The message was signed 'R.C.'

This message began a two-month period of vigilantism by the Royal Charmers. It was a campaign in which one dealer was pushed off a roof, his dead body found weeks later in an alley garbage can, two others were murdered, junkies were whipped through South Bronx streets, and one Royal Charmer was blinded, the victim of a shotgun blast in the face from a vengeful drug dealer.

The Savage Nomads demonstrate an early take on up-rocking in this publicity photo used for the release Gary Weiss' 80 Blocks from Tiffany's. *By today's standards the gangs of this era seem almost innocent, although in truth, this is the generation that developed the worship of random acts of violence. Weiss treated graffiti as part of the gang culture, when, it fact, it was developing a separate and much different code based more on the lone warrior against the system. And even though the rap scene was peaking, Weiss hung exclusively with an already fading streetgang culture, when he could have been filming the classic battles between the Furious and the Funky Four.*

Contrary to the myth created by this and other articles, street gangs did not appear in the Bronx solely to rid the streets of junkies. Junkies just happened to be the first convenient target of some newly formed gangs that wanted to flex a little muscle: They were easy to identify, they had no potential as gang members, and they could be beaten up without arousing a cry of anguish from the community. Gang leaders were also smart enough to realize that heroin was one of the major reasons why the Bronx remained pacified throughout the sixties.

As the gang culture spread through the city, several hundred new gangs were formed. Most were dominated by four members: the president, the vice-president, the warlord (who attended pow-wows with rival gangs and declared war if necessary), and the masher, the best street fighter. The gangs had clubhouses where weekly meetings were held, and ritualistic initiation rites, the most common of which was called "Running the Mill," a rite of passage that required new members to run between two rows of members wielding chains, pipes, and studded belts. Every gang had the same uniform: Jean jackets with insignias on the back, Lee jeans, Garrison belts, and engineer boots. Lists of rules and regulations were drawn up and severely adhered to. It was easy to join and hard to quit.

The number of gangs in the Bronx kept growing through the summer of 1971, but this development went largely unnoticed until Adlai E. Stevenson High School re-opened its doors in September. Located in the North Bronx, Stevenson was a new school located in a predominately white neighborhood. During its second year the school started receiving busloads of blacks and Hispanics from the South Bronx, as well as a sizeable contingent of whites from middle-class neighborhoods in Throgs Neck and Pelham Bay.

Afrika Bambaataa, who would later become a leader in the largest gang in the city, was in the eighth grade when he was bused to Stevenson. He recalled the first two weeks of school in a lengthy history he wrote for English class titled *Street Gangs Beware*:

For the first week things seemed to go okay. There were no sign of a gang or gang activities in the school, not until a couple of Black Spades and Savage Nomads started flying colors in the second week. Then other gang members from a variety of streetgangs started wearing their colors. Suddenly, Stevenson officials found out that at least a member from every streetgang in the Bronx and parts of Manhattan went to Stevenson High School. Tension arose between the black and Hispanic against the whites. There was all kinds of trouble happening. A couple of white teenagers had a fight with a black who happened to be in the Black Spades. After school was over, the Black Spades led an army of students to the Korvettes Shopping Center where the white teenagers catch the #5 bus to Throgs Neck/Pelham Bay area. A rumble broke out...A white got thrown through a window and other whites and blacks and Hispanics got stabbed and stomped. After that day Stevenson was never the same peaceful high school again.

Several predominantly white gangs had been formed in the North Bronx, including the Aliens, the Golden Guineas, and the War Pigs, but after the fight at Stevenson they merged into a single gang called Ministers Bronx. Violence in the school became an everyday occurrence. Many students refused to eat lunch in the cafeteria, where fights were likely to break out. All the bathrooms but a few had to be locked permanently; those that remained open had guards posted at the doors.

Bambaataa joined the Black Spades in 1969, shortly after a division was founded at the Bronx River Project, where he lived with his mother. Although he became a devoted member, Bambaataa was far from a typical one. While the others were out playing basketball or hanging around street corners, Bambaataa was scouring record bins for obscure rhythm & blues recordings. Just as unusual was the name he chose for himself, which was inspired by the release of a feature film about the Zulus, a fierce, warrior tribe in Africa. The original Bambaataa was a Zulu chief at the turn of the century. Translated into English, the word means "affectionate leader."

"Bam was never interested in sports. As long as I've known him, he's always been the music man," said Jay McGluery, who grew up at Bronx River with Bambaataa. "His mother was a nurse and she was constantly on the go, so we always went to his house to party. He had every record you could want to hear, including a lot of rock albums. James Brown and Sly and the Family Stone was his favorites."

In his many snapshots from the period, Bambaataa looks young, lean, and angry, his eyebrows fused in a permanent scowl of disapproval—just the sort of look designed to intimidate whitey. Despite the angry look, he tended to be quiet and philosophical, his guarded, reserved air frequently shattered by a laugh so friendly it infected everyone around him.

He was also more attuned to politics than many of his fellow gang members, some of whom understood only three basic concepts: "crush, kill and destroy." When he was twelve, he had already begun hanging out at the Black Panther Information Center. His political leanings were encouraged by the appearance of *Say it Loud, I'm Black and I'm Proud* by James Brown and *Stand* by Sly and the Family Stone.

However, like many gang members, Bambaataa had a reckless, unpredictable streak. One time he and McGluery were playing war games and McGluery took refuge in one of the project's apartment buildings. Bambaataa poured gasoline on the sidewalk in front of the building, lit it, and announced he was holding everyone hostage. That same summer, he convinced his friends to buy target bows and arrows so they could hunt rabbits on the banks of the Bronx River. "Bam was always a leader," said McGluery. "He was always full of crazy ideas."

During the early seventies, life at Bronx River changed dramatically. Since it was a stronghold for gang activity, the project was under constant police surveillance. Any teenager wearing engineer boots was likely to be stopped for a grilling, which usually started with the question "Are you a Spade or a Skull?" (the two largest gangs in the area). It was not unusual for fistfights to break out between gang members and the police. Since the police were almost entirely white at the time, charges of police racism were rampant. Considering that newspaper stories from the period indicate that white gang members were seldom arrested, the charges may have had some foundation.

Although several rumbles were arranged between the Black Spades and the Ministers, they were usually aborted. The Spades couldn't board a bus headed uptown without it being surrounded by squad cars before it reached the Ministers' turf. Typically, the windows of the bus would fly open and a shower of chains, knives, bats, and zip guns would hit the pavement. On June 27, 1973, a brief battle was broken up by police in front of P.S. 127 on Castle Hill Avenue, resulting in the arrest of eighteen Black Spades.

Gang activity tended to quiet down during the winter only to resurface with even greater intensity each summer. Every year the gangs seemed to fall under the control of older, more demented individuals, many of whom were returning from stints in prison. By 1972, Runing the Mill was being replaced by gang rape.

STREET GANG RAPES GIRL IN BRONX

(New York Post, November 9, 1973)
A 16-year-old cheerleader on her way home from practice at Evander Childs HS was abducted by members of a Bronx sreet gang and raped and beaten.
In another incident only hours earlier yesterday afternoon, a 15-year-old girl was abducted off the street, raped and beaten at gunpoint in a Brooklyn apartment, police said.
In the Bronx incident, the girl told police she was abducted around 4:45 P.M. by four youths in a car as she was walking near 212th St. and White Plains Road, four blocks from school.
She was blindfolded and taken to an apartment building in the Hunts Point section that police suspect was a clubhouse of the Black Spades, a Bronx street gang.
According to the account given police, the girl, whose name was withheld, was raped in the apartment by three youths and hit several times with bottles and chukka sticks—lengths of wood slung from rope or cord.
The girl said she was blindfolded again and driven to a deserted area at 151st St. and River Ave., where she was forced to commit sodomy with at least seven other youths.

Violence between gangs intensified as well. One feud between the Black Spades and the Seven Crowns lasted for 92 days, during which time the Bronx River Project was constantly peppered with gunfire from passing cars. Shootouts became so common that the residents started calling it "Li'l Vietnam."

"I was into street gang violence," admitted Bambaataa. "That was all part of growing up in the Southeast Bronx." However, that's about all he'll say on the subject. "I don't really be speaking on that stuff because it's negative," he explained. "The Black Spades was also helping out in the community, raising money for sickle cell anemia and getting people to register to vote."

"He was not what I would call gung-ho," added McGluery, who became warlord of the Bronx River division before quitting to join the Marines. "Bam was more like a supervisor. There were so many different gangs and he knew at least five members in every one. Any time there was a conflict, he would try and straighten it out. He was into communications."

Black Spade circa 1970 by Richard Sisco: engineer boots, cut-off jean vest with insignia on back, flair-bottom jeans and garrison belt.

Gang activity probably peaked in 1973, when there were an estimated 315 gangs in the city, claiming 19,503 members. The Black Spades were by far the largest and most feared, with a divison in almost every precinct. However, by 1974, the Black Spades began to disintegrate.

"Some gangs got into drugs," said Bambaataa. "Other gangs got wiped out by other gangs. Others got so big that members didn't want to be involved no more. Girls got tired of it first. They wanted to have children. Plus times was changin'. The seventies was coming more into music and dancing and going to clubs. The lifestyle was changing."

After many of the original Black Spades were killed, jailed or dropped out of the gang, Bambaataa took on an increasingly influential role. His affiliation continued until January 10, 1975, when his best friend, Soulski, was shot and killed by two policemen on Pelham Parkway. Bambaataa insisted that the shooting was nothing short of an assassination carried out during a police crackdown on gang activity. A Xerox of his friend's death certificate hangs in his bedroom. "He got shot in about nine different places," said Bambaataa. "The back, the stomach, the face. At first, I wanted to go to war with the police, but we couldn't really win. *The Amsterdam News* calmed everybody down and told us to fight through the system. It went to trial, but the cops never got convicted."

For over five years the Bronx had lived in constant terror of streetgangs. Then, in the summer of 1976, they unexpectedly failed to appear. Something better had come along to replace the gangs.

Chapter 2: The War of Words

You know what *it evolved from? The toughest guy on the block always had his name the biggest in the street. It told everybody it was his area, that he had the juice to do what he wanted and nobody could mess with him.—Tracy 168*

To tell the truth, nobody really knows how graffiti evolved—we just know it's been around for a long time. During World War II, a welding inspector at the Bethlehem Steel shipyard in Quincy, Massachusetts, named James J. Kilroy began writing "Kilroy was here" in crayon inside ships that were being built for the war. Many servicemen saw the markings and began spreading his message throughout Europe and the United States. Eventually, the phrase was combined with a drawing on a long-nosed face peering over a wall. Kilroy spreaders would sometimes draw mustaches on advertising posters and write additional obscenities to complement the message. The New York City subway system became one of their favorite doodling spots.

In the fifties, street gangs used graffiti for self-promotion and marking territorial boundaries. Gang graffiti had other uses, such as intimidation. When rival gangs walked into a new area and saw "Savage Skulls" written a hundred times—each with a different name underneath—it told them the Skulls were a powerful force to be reckoned with.

But then something changed. Around 1969, graffiti became more that a gang-related activity or a thoughtless moment of vandalism. For hundreds of New York City teenagers it became a way of life with its own codes of behavior, secret gathering places, slang, and esthetic standards. No one knows who started it. We only know who made it famous: TAKI 183.

Taki 183: the original "king" of New York City graffiti, photo by Andre Grossmann.

His real name was Demetrius and he came to New York from Greece. His family moved to Washington Heights, a working-class neighborhood at the northern edge of Manhattan. Demetrius was fifteen when an older boy in the neighborhood told him about the gangs from the 1950s. "They had an initiation where they would hang a new member by his ankles off the side of a bridge," said Demetrius. "While hanging upside down, the guy would paint his name on a pillar. I never saw it done, but the idea interested me."

Graffiti writing got a big technological boost in the sixties with the invention of the magic market, which was easy to conceal and, like spray paint, left an indelible mark on just about any surface. In 1967, Demetrius noticed the name "JULIO 204" written on the street around his house. Julio, who lived a couple of blocks away on 204th Street, like to write his name and street number wherever he went. Demetrius lived on 183rd Street and his nickname was Taki. So he started writing TAKI 183.

He put his first "tag" on the side of an ice-cream truck during the summer of 1970. "I didn't have a job. I did it to pass time," he said later. Meanwhile, Julio was arrested for vandalism and forced into early retirement. When Taki returned to school, he got a part-time job as a messenger. While making deliveries, he found an art supply store on 53rd Street that sold extra-wide markers. "I think I was the first one to find that wide marker," he said. "My name got noticed because it was wider than everyone else's. But even more important, I was writing in a different area than most people. My name could have been on every street corner in Brooklyn and I wouldn't have gotten the exposure I got from writing on the East Side. A writer might come out of his office, see my name, and—maybe because it was a boring day—he would decide to write a story about me."

Taki graduated from high school and began working full time until he saved enough money to attend college. He continued writing, only now the interiors of subway cars had become his primary target. People have nothing to do in subway trains except read the advertising posters, he reasoned, so why not give them a little something extra to look at?

Unknowingly, Taki created a major controversy. "Pretty soon people were wondering, what is the squad of Taki-commandos?" wrote Richard Goldstein in *New York* magazine. "Rumors began: Is it the surveying crew for a new subway line, or is it a madman quoting stock averages, or is it a street gang so obscure not even Leonard Bernstein knows them, or else is it some kind of arcane religious rite, like when I was a kid and people went around writing 'Beware on 1960' on the roofs?" The controversy was finally settled in July 1971, when an enterprising reporter from

The New York Times tracked Taki down. The first newspaper article on graffiti appeared a few days later.

TAKI 183' SPAWNS PEN PALS

Taki is a Manhattan teenager who writes his name and his street number everywhere he goes. He says it is something he just has to do.

His TAKI 183 appears in subway stations and inside subway cars all over the city, on wall along Broadway, at Kennedy International Airport, in New Jersey, Connecticut, upstate New York and other places.

He has spawned hundreds of imitators, including JOE 136, BARBARA 62, EEL 159, YANQUI 135 and LEO 136.

To remove such words, plus the obscenities and other graffiti in subway stations, it cost 80,000 man-hours, or about $300,000, in the last year, the Transit Authority estimates.
"I work, I pay taxes too and it doesn't harm anybody," Taki said in an interview, when told the cost of removing the graffiti.

And he asked: "Why do they go after the little guy? Why not the campaign organizations that put stickers all over the subways at election time?"

It was apparent that Taki had gained considerable status in his community for the graffiti. "He's the king," said one neighborhood youth. "He's got everybody doing it," said another. After the article appeared, Taki's status was no longer confined to his block, but stretched to every borough in the city, including the Bronx.

Actually, the Bronx had been writing similar graffiti long before the article on Taki appeared. However, it wasn't until the spring of 1971 that the fad began taking off. In March, two writers appeared on 163rd Street, SLY II and LEE 163rd!. Lee drew immediate attention for his unusual tag, which stacked and fused the letters in his name into a corporate-style logo, ending with an exclamation mark.

In October Lee's cousin, Lonny Wood, began writing. "The previous year we'd given this party," said Lonny. "We were getting ready to give another one and I said, 'We'll call it Phase Two.' I don't know why, but I was stuck on the name. It had meaning for me. I started writing 'Phase 2.'

By this time, the unspoken graffiti code was already well established. Writers were supposed to be mysterious figures who never revealed their identity to outsiders (especially parents). They had to be light-fingered enough to steal markers and spray paint, and courageous enough to "run the train tracks" and participate in other daredevil stunts.

"We were like moles," said Tracy 168, one of the first writers to appear in the Bronx. "If anyone chased us, we ran into the nearest subway station and we'd be gone. Nobody would follow us down there." It took considerable nerve to jump off a subway platform and take off running down a dark, forbidding tunnel. The third rail, pulsing with 625 deadly volts, was just a stumble away. Somewhere behind the writer, moving at 40 miles an hour or faster, was a subway train, while perhaps a thousand feet in front was an abandoned station or lay-up track, where the writer could leave a tag, like a flag driven into a mountain peak. It was criminal, dangerous behavior, but the thrill was undeniable.

Phase 2 joined a large number of writers at DeWitt Clinton High School. One advantage to attending Clinton was the proximity of a Transit Authority storage yard across the street, where parked trains could be found any time of day or night. It wasn't unusual for Phase and the other writers to spend their lunch hour in the yard marking up trains. After school the writers would gather in a nearby coffee shop. Whenever a bus pulled up outside, dozens of writers came pouring out of the coffee shop waving markers. By the time the bus pulled away, it would be drenched in freshly scrawled signatures.

At first there were only a handful of writers in each neighborhood, and it didn't matter what a tag looked like. But after hundreds of writers appeared on the scene, it was necessary to embellish the tags to make them stand out. Two female writers, Barbara and Eva 62, enlarged their signatures and made them more colorful. Cay 161 drew a crown over his tag. Stay High 149 drew a stick figure with a halo smoking a joint.

In 1973, the first serious book about New York City graffiti was published and it included a text by Norman Mailer, who, unfortunately, did little research, although the many photographs from the book remain some of the best examples of the early years of the subculture.

Graffiti began to draw the scrutiny of outsiders, most of whom assumed it was done out of anger and frustration. "It is part of the widespread vandalism, the mood to destroy, the brutalism that is everywhere," said Dr. Fredric Wertham. Mayor John Lindsay denounced the writers as "insecure cowards" and launched an all-out campaign to remove graffiti from public property.

In 1981, filmmaker Manny Kirchheimer produced an elegant ode to New York subway graffiti, all set to a score by Charles Mingus; titled **Stations of the Elevated***, it represented the first time a filmmaker presented a serious take on the subculture as an expression of legitimate folk art instead of pointless vandalism.*

Although the writers continued to hit buses, handball courts, schoolyards, and other locations, the subway system was the primary target. "One thing that kept me writing on trains was seeing my name again," said Tracy. "You thought your tag would just disappear because there were so many trains. But then it would come back the next day, and you'd see somebody else's tag right next to yours. That was part of the communication thing. The train would shoot over to Brooklyn and somebody over there would see your style. But there was also more adventure on the trains. Daredevil stunts like jumping from trains to platforms would really get your adrenaline going. Competition was important too."

The writers soon moved from marking the insides of trains to marking the exteriors. It was decided the best place to have a tag was on the front of the train, where it would be the first thing seen as the train entered the station. But in 1972, Super Kool completely changed graffiti by spray-painting his name in super-wide pink and yellow letters. It took him about five times longer than a normal tag, and used almost an entire can of paint, but the results were worth it. His thick, colorful letters overpowered every other signature on the train. At first the other writers couldn't figure out how Super Kool had gotten his letters so thick. It didn't seem possible with a regular can of spray paint, and, in fact, it wasn't. Super Kool had replaced the narrow-dispersion cap on his spray-paint can with a wider-spraying cap from a can of oven cleaner.

Phase 2 in 1983, photo by Steven Hager.

"Everyone was damn negative about it at first," said Phase. "It took a whole can of paint for one signature! But then everybody picked up on it. I remember seeing some big block letters by Sentry. That's when I came out with my softie letters. People started calling it the bubble style."

The giant signatures became known as "masterpieces" and it suddenly became necessary to steal a lot of paint to execute them.

"Super Kool and his girl friend were the first to rack up huge quantities," said Phase. "He always dressed very dapper and didn't look the part. Stealing went along with the graffiti style. I didn't get into it, but a lot of guys did. Not just paint, but leather coats, stereos. One time I led about twenty guys into a store. We went straight to the paint. Something came over me and I slapped all the cans on the shelf. It was crazy. There was so much confusion. The salesman tried to keep us in the store and guys had to throw blows to get out. The mounted police came. We ran around the corner and found we had four cans of paint between twenty guys. That wasn't the way to do it."

Like most writers in the Bronx, Phase was black. He was tall, skinny, and almost always wore a hat jauntily perched on one side of his head—a French cap made by Flechet was his favorite. He projected an almost explosive sense of urgency, his occasional stuttering heightening the impression that his physical being was struggling to keep pace with a hyperactive imagination. While talking, he frequently twisted and clenched his fingers, as if creating patterns for some bizarre new lettering style.

Style became the most important aspect of graffiti. It was still possible to gain respect and recognition merely by "getting one's name around" in large quantities, but it was more prestigious to create original lettering styles that were imitated by lesser writers, who were known as "toys." One had to be artistically competent to execute huge murals on the sides of trains. The less talented writers were forced out of the limelight. Meanwhile, the Transit Authority continued cracking down on graffiti and it became progressively more difficult and dangerous to enter the train yards. However, the danger only increased the writers' sense of satisfaction.

A writer named Top Cat moved to New York from Philadelphia, where a separate graffiti subculture was flourishing. Top Cat painted thin, elongated letters on platforms. He called it the "Philadelphia style," but after the letters were imitated by most of the writers on the Upper West Side, they were renamed "Broadway elegant."

Although most writers tended to be fairly independent, it wasn't long before they began gathering in loose-knit groups, which were closer to professional associations than gangs. Meetings were held at various "writers' corners" around the city, the two most prominent of which were located at a subway station at 149th Street and the Grand Concourse in the Bronx, and on the corner of 188th and Audubon Avenue in Manhattan. Wherever they gathered, writers compared notes on various lettering styles and discussed methods for thwarting the Transit Police.

The Ex-Vandals, one of the earliest and most revered of the writing organizations, were founded at Erasmus High School in Brooklyn by president Dino Nod, whose tag could be found in every borough of the city. The name was short for "Experienced Vandals." In imitation of the street gangs, the Ex-Vandals wore jean jackets with their name on the back. They were not a fighting gang, however. They preferred to spend their time developing highly elaborate, script-like tags. It was the beginning of the Brooklyn style, which eventually became so complex most people found it indecipherable.

Phase became president of the Bronx chapter of the Ex-Vandals until he founded a separate group called "The Independent Writers," whose membership included such prominent writers as Super Kool and Stay High. Independent writers indicated their affiliation by writing "INDS" after their signature.

Wanted, another important writing group, was founded by Tracy 168 in 1972. Tracy was a gutsy, streetwise white kid, tough enough to hang out with the Black Spades in his neighborhood.

Unlike many of the other groups, Wanted had a permanent clubhouse, in the basement of an apartment complex on the corner of 166th Street and Woodycrest Avenue in the Bronx. In the mid-seventies, Wanted became one of the largest groups, with more than 70 members.

"The best year for graffiti was 1973," said Tracy. "Styles were coming out. We got into this thing with colors. First it was two colors, then three colors, then four. Then it was the biggest piece, the widest. Then it was top-to-bottom, whole car, whole train. We worked on clouds and flames. We got into lettering. Everybody was trying to develop their own techniques. When I would go into a yard, the first thing I'd do is look around and see who was good. That would be my objective. To burn the best writer in the yard. And I wouldn't leave until I did something better than him. I put a Yosemite Sam with two guns on a piece. That was the first cartoon character."

Although Phase wasn't painting as many trains as some other writers, he was inventing new styles on paper and handing them out to his friends. Many of his ideas found their way to the trains through Riff 170, who was considered a master colorist. "Riff revolutionized graffiti with a half-car, top-to-bottom," said Aaron 155, interviewed by Craig Castleman in *Getting Up.*

"It was a yellow 'Riff' with red, bloody drips coming down. And it had cracks painted on it. It took everybody out all over New York."

Other important writing groups included: Magic Inc., Three Yard Boys, Vanguards, Ebony Dukes, Writers Corner 188, The Bad Artists, the Mad Bombers, the Death Squad, Mission Graffiti, the Rebels, Wild Style, Six Yard Boys, and the Crazy 5. Many writers belonged to two or three at the same time.

Although Soul Artists was not a major group in the early seventies, it was founded by Mark Edmonds and Lennie McGurr, who would become well known in the eighties. The two were best friends through grade school and organized the Soul Artists in 1972, while working as gym instructors for the West Side YMCA. "At first we'd hit anything—buildings, cars, trucks," said Edmonds, who wrote "ALI." "Then after a while, we told the members that anyone signing the club initials S.A., to anything but trains would be thrown out. To join, people had to submit designs. We really wanted good artists and we would help each other developing techniques."

When Ali was 16, he earned a scholarship to study urban planning at Columbia University. He was black, handsome, and possessed a quick wit. McGurr, who wrote "Futura 2000," was not a natural leader like Ali, but showed greater potential as an artist. He was adopted as a child and looked somewhat Puerto Rican. Futura graduated from a trade school specializing in the printing industry and took his tag from the name of a typeface. After he left school, he got a job at a McDonald's restaurant.

At 5 A.M. on the morning of October 8, 1973, Futura and Ali were standing on a train track north of the IRT station at 137th and Broadway. While they were painting a parked train, another train began moving slowly toward them. They crawled under the train they were painting to wait for the moving train to pass. Suddenly, the train they were sitting under also started up. They quickly crawled back onto the track.

"Ali had about twenty cans of paint with him in a sack," said Chris Pape, a former member of the Soul Artists, who's tag was the revolutionary-tinged: Freedom. "One of the cans had a faulty nozzle that was spraying paint. A spark from the train ignited the cans just as Ali was diving back on the tracks. Ali jumped right over the explosion and was set on fire. Not only was he on fire, but he had no place to go. There was a train moving toward him, so he couldn't lie down and put himself out. Right here is where the story gets confusing. Does Futura put out the fire? Or does he run away? The way I think it happened is that Futura heard the explosion, but didn't know Ali was on fire. He went, 'Oh, shit!' and ran back to the platform. Then Futura saw Ali all burnt up, helped him out of the station, and flagged a cab. The word on the street was that Futura had run out on Ali and betrayed him. I felt bad for him 'cause there were a lot of former friends out to kill him. The boys from 105th Street—where Futura lived—were ready to curb stomp him. To this day nobody really knows what happened."

While still in the hospital, Ali was interviewed by a reporter from the *New York Times*. "He is immobile, in pain, confused and contrite, and he wanted to tell his story and the story of the graffiti subculture in the hope of discouraging others from doing what he now says is 'crazy, stupid and too damn dangerous." ...his best friend abandoned him and that memory adds to his pain," wrote Michael T. Kaufman.

The article created the impression that Futura had left Ali in the tunnel to die, a serious violation of the graffiti code. "I don't know why he said those things," said Futura several years later. "I took off my jacket, put out the fire, and helped him to the hospital. But after that story came out, things got pretty heavy for me around the neighborhood." Futura had to get away, so he joined the Navy. Soul Artists disbanded. The accident caused a few writers to quit graffiti but it had little effect on most of the subculture.

Eventually, someone from the outside had to stumble across graffiti, realize that something more than mindless vandalism was going on, and try to refocus the energies and talents of the subculture into more legitimate enterprises. That person was Hugo Martinez, a sociology major at City College. In 1972 Martinez spent the summer working with streetgangs as part of a federally funded program at Queens College. When returned to school that fall, his interest in youth groups continued. He heard about the graffiti subculture from a fellow student and set out for Washington Heights, a known hangout for writers. He met Freddie 173, who provided a tour of the neighborhood.

"The tour climaxed at 'Writer's Corner 188,' a wall at 188th Street and Audubon Avenue," wrote Martinez in the first graffiti-art catalog." Freddie formally introduced me to the president and vice-president of the site, Stitch I and Snake I, along with CAT 87. They received me with silent suspicion and an air of being used to admiration, of expecting it. Stitch was wearing a black fishing hat, black leather buttoned-down jacket, dark gray beat-up pants, and Pro-Keds. Snake wore a red corduroy jacket, Levis, and Pro-Keds. They had founded Writer's Corner, converting the pink wall of the building into a tapestry of line and color. Here the best writers of Manhattan, the Bronx, and Brooklyn would come to meet, sign in, exchange gossip and, if the feelings were right, go out and hit together. Here also toy (inexperienced, inadequate) writers could look upon their heroes and perhaps get their autographs. (Only the best writers of Manhattan were allowed to consider themselves privileged to add 'W.C. 188' to their signatures.)"

In October, Martinez arranged for twelve writers to come to City College for a graffiti-writing demonstration. He covered an entire 10-by-40-foot wall with wrapping paper and brought dozens of cans of spray paint. "They came armed with their own markers, ranging from 1/4-inch 'toy markers' to 2-inch 'Uni-wides,'" wrote Martinez. "Once they realized all the possibilities, all vestiges of street cool went out the window. They were ecstatic. The presence of so many master together, all the spray paint, and so much room to hit created a scene of controlled frenzy."

Phase 2: Evolution of a style, 1971 to 1976:

Later that month, Martinez founded United Graffit Artists (UGA), a quasi-democratic organization designed to redirect the efforts of the elite writers. At first the group was entirely Puerto Rican—with the exception of one Greek. Since they respected the work of the Bronx writers, many Puerto Ricans wanted to admit writers like Phase 2, Super Kool, and Lee 163rd!. Martinez was widely accused of racism because he didn't allow blacks into UGA.

"Three or four members did not want to accept blacks," Martinez said later. "I tried to manipulate votes and put pressure on certain individuals to bring them into the group." Within a few months the Bronx writers were admitted, but some felt they were being accorded second-class status. "I think he favored the Puerto Ricans," said Lee 163rd! "Sometimes he would hold meetings with them and we wouldn't find out until later."

One thing is certain: There was a tremendous amount of racial tension at UGA, which was unusual since most writers respected one another regardless of color. The tension eventually flared into a full-scale rumble at the new headquarters on Jumel Place and 168th Street. Henry 161 shoed up one day accompanied by five members of the Young Galaxies, a local street gang. They immediately began trashing the studio. "I got hit in the head with a stick," said Phase 2. "So did Hugo. I later found out certain writers felt threatened by us. Henry got kicked out of the group."

There were other problems, like the controversy between Snake I and Snake 131. Snake 131 was considered the original Snake and to prove it, he started writing "SNAKE I-131." It was too much for Snake I to bear. One day he showed up at Snake 131's house, accompanied by his friend Stitch, who packed a gun and was considered one of the toughest street fighters in the neighborhood. When Snake 131 opened the door, Stitch had only four terse words for him: "Drop the fucking one." Stitch and Snake I spun on their heels and left. From that day on, Snake 131 never wrote an extra one.

Martinez may not have been very effective at unifying the writers, but his appreciation for their work was obviously sincere. His analysis of the typical writer's economic background was perceptive and still holds true today. "All the masters were working-class offspring from working-class neighborhoods like Washington Heights, West Bronx, and Flatbush," he wrote. "The hardcore poor of the Lower East Side, South Bronx, and Brownsville—those from homes where neither parent works—did not create ambitious graffiti. The masters were 'good kids' whose parents worked for a living and participated in the American dream of becoming middle-class. The bitterness and self-recrimination that permeate the poor were absent from their environments. Among the black families, it was not uncommon to find private houses, a car, color TV; in the Latino homes these articles were definite goals. High-school and even college educations were fostered aspirations."

Blue Magic by Richard Admiral (AMRL, BAMA) spray paint on canvas, 7 x 12', 1974.

Martinez organized the first graffiti art exhibition at City College's Eisner Hall in December 1972. Publicity for the show landed a commission from choreographer Twyla Tharp, who wanted graffiti-style backdrops for her production of *Deuce Coupe*. The following year The Razor Gallery exhibited 20 giant canvases by UGA members. Media attention given to the show was overwhelming: Feature stories appeared in several newspapers,

Newsweek provided a splashy, two-page spread, and droves of art critics appeared at the opening. However, praise for the work was hardly universal.

"The show-off ebullience of their work has, if anything, been heightened by the comforts of a studio situation," wrote Peter Schjeldahl in *The New York Times*. "It is too much to say, however, that any of them is yet a really accomplished artist. All are understandably weak in terms of structure; at best, their canvasses tend to look like segments of something bigger rather than whole compositions. They really have trouble with small pictures, most of which resemble pep-less, overelaborate doodles. But raw talent abounds."

Personality problems continued to plague the group. According to some members, Martinez attempted to manipulate the direction of the work, refusing to exhibit paintings that did not conform to his idea of "good" graffiti. Charges of racism were still leveled at Martinez, who continued to hold segments of some meetings in Spanish. the writers were invited to come to Chicago for the exhibit at the Museum of Science and Industry. When they returned to New York, the membership seized control of the organization and demoted Martinez from "director" to "advisor."

The 1975 art season opened in New York with a spectacular graffiti-art exhibit at the Artist Space gallery in SoHo. By this time Phase and Bama had clearly emerged as the most talented artists in the $1,000-to-$3,000 price range. However, the event failed to attract media attention comparable to the previous shows. The group was losing its momentum. Whatever his faults, Martinez was obviously an important motivating force behind UGA. Without his guidance, the organization soon split apart and went underground, leaving the galleries to return to the subway yards. It would be five years before the subculture regained the prominence in the art world that it had in 1975—and then it would be riding the coattails of the sudden, unexpected commercial success of rap music.

Hyperbolic Paranoia, by Lonny Wood (Phase 2, CAD) spray paint on canvas, 6 x 16', 1974.

"I grew up in an atmosphere where we recognized we were being robbed of knowledge of culture and knowledge of self, says Phase 2 today. "We created an art form that came up from our supposedly insignificant existences and now it's everywhere on earth. That's a testament in itself. In the late 1960's amidst an abundance of political and social turmoil, cultural awareness, racial pride and unrest, a youth-inspired movement emerged. Those who spawned its birth called it "writing." Writing and the aerosol art movement as we know it today, its elements, its hows, its whys, began in New York City all by it's lonesome and was never influenced by any other so-called writer movements anywhere else on the planet earth. If we didn't do it here it wouldn't exist as you are witnessing it. I'm not trying to disrespect or toot my own horn but I was always doing my thing. For example, I danced. I could draw. I played b-ball. I was under 6-foot-tall just before my 15th birthday dunking above regulation rims. The school system deemed me smarter than average. I'm not ego-tripping and I don't concoct stories. I'm just trying to make a point. I didn't need my name on a subway car to tell me that I was a bit nice.

'The name of the game was getting up. I started doing it because someone I rolled with on the daily was down with it. So many guys created and developed a signature and name to suit them and be original and independent. You could easily see some type of a personality or flavor in the signatures of a Super Kool 223 or a Jec Star, Cay 161, LEE 163d!, Slim one, Kool Kito, King Of Kools, Dino Nod, Tye 24. Some of these names seemed resounding and the signatures were in their own way no less then dignified and quite amazing.

'Writing had guidelines, rules and regulations. Respect the name. No writing over one another. Start nothing there'll be nothing. Don't mess with me; I won't mess with you. So we had ethics. I seem to have always connected to the things that I could elaborate and innovate off of. Dancing. Drawing. Balling. You could always flip it how you wanted to.

'You have to think what if there was no Super Kool or Riff 170? Would there be the masterpieces on trains, top to bottoms, fat caps, ill designs, certain funky styles or what?

'What you see these days was basically blueprinted in the 1970's. The technical aspects are different, but there's no way that you could have any of this without the signature and style formations that were done then. In the 1980's, you had major developments like Futura's spray can technology and what came out of the West Coast with guys like Slic and Hex that changed the whole approach to technique and that has also become a staple in the culture. Almost like a second blueprint that has also been adapted globally. It all started with little magic markers. And developed into something way out-of-control and much bigger than that. We're a part of something that is not only a part of New York history...but a part of the world. Instead of trying to deal with the culture, the authorities chose to wipe it out. Just think...they tried to kill it, but it just wouldn't die."

There was one very important writer Martinez had failed to recruit, however: Stay High 149. Aside from Phase 2, Stay High was the most influential writer of his generation, as well as the most mysterious. His tag appeared in the most amazing places and carried a style all its own. He was also a bit of a revolutionary in that a political statement about marijuana legalization seemed to play a role in his work. Stay High usually included a stick figure taken from *The Saint* TV show, who was depicted smoking a joint. The "H" in "High" also appeared as a smoking joint. Everybody knew Stay High was one of the greatest writers in terms of pure calligraphy, as well his ability to get-up and establish his title of one of the "kings," but Stay High's whereabouts and true identity were remained unknown to most. Meanwhile, one of Stay High's original writing partners, Kool Herc was about to emerge as the godfather of hip hop music.

Chapter 3: Herculords at the Hevalo

Since Clive Campbell's impressions of the United States had been formed watching *Dennis the Menace* and *Bewitched* on his next-door neighbor's television set in Kingston, Jamaica, it was easy to understand why he thought the country was so clean, without a trace of garbage anywhere. So it came as something of a shock when, at age 12, Clive landed at Kennedy airport and took the bus to his mother's apartment on 168th Street. It was 1967. Rather than clean suburban lawns, he found a ghetto similar to the one in Kingston—only bigger.

Kool Herc in 1983, photograph by Stephen Crichlow.

Clive had a lot of trouble adjusting to the Bronx. His accent made him sound like a hick and his main sports in Jamaica—soccer and bicycle racing—weren't at all popular. Instead, everyone was playing basketball. The first day Clive tried the sport, he got kicked by an angry teammate. "I knew how to kick," he said, "so I kicked him right back. A fight started. Two members of the Five Percenters [a Black Muslim youth group] came to my rescue. They weren't gonna let anybody dog me. I hung out with them and started picking up the slang. Pretty soon, I was Americanized."

In 1970, Clive entered Alfred E. Smith High School, a trade school for auto mechanics. He began lifting weights and running on the track team. A friend nicknamed him Hercules for his well-developed body. "I resented the name," he said. "I broke it down to Herc. That sounded rare, so I kept it." That same year, Herc started hanging out at a disco called the Plaza Tunnel, which was located in the basement of the Plaza Hotel on 161st Street and the Grand Concourse. The deejay, John Brown, was the first to play records like *Give It Up or Turn It Loose* by James Brown and *Get Ready* by Rare Earth. Unfortunately, the Black Spades liked to drop by unexpectedly to steal girl friends, rough up rival gang members, and generally intimidate the crowd. When they arrived, Brown tried to pacify them by playing *Soul Power* by James Brown. They loved chanting "Spade Power! Spade Power!" along with the record.

"I was known as a graffiti writer," said Herc. "I also ran the 880 relay on the track team, dressed well and danced. *Get Ready* was my favorite song. But then the music stopped. I think the gangs stopped it. It got too dangerous for people to go to discos."

In 1973 Herc's sister Cindy celebrated her birthday by throwing a party in the recreation room at a housing project on Sedgwick Avenue. "She asked me to provide the music," said Herc, "so I went out and bought all the fresh, up-to-date records. I rigged a little hook-up with two turntables. All our friends came to the party along with a lot of people from the neighborhood. I played songs like *Give It Up or Turn It Loose*. People would walk for miles just to hear that record—because nobody could find it." The party was such a success that Herc continued deejaying at house parties and community centers. He collected a trunk full of dance 45s and invested in better equipment, including a mike with an echo chamber and strobe light. Later that year, he began charging a 25-cent entrance fee.

"I was twelve the first time I went to Herc's party," said Kevin, who became one of the original b-boys. "My brother Keith and I used to hang out with some girls around 165th Street and

University Avenue and they kept saying: 'Y'all should come to Herc's! It's a party and he's jamming every week!' One night we decided to check it out. The thing I mostly remember was how loud the music was. The sound overtook you. The place was packed—a real sweatbox. Herc was on the mike. He'd say things like 'Rock the house' and call out the names of people at the party. Wallace Dee, Johnny Cool, Chubby, the Amazing Bobo, James Bond, Sa-sa, Clark Kent, Trixie—those were the names you heard. Trixie had a big afro and he used to shake his head. It used to make him look so good! Wallace Dee had a move called the slingshot, which was a basic drop to the floor except he came up like he was shooting a slingshot. After that first time, we didn't want to go anywhere else. It was Kool Herc's, Kool Herc's, Kool Herc's. Every weekend. There was no such thing as b-boys when we arrived, but Herc gave us that tag. Just like he named his sound system the Herculords and he called me and my brother the Nigger Twins. He called his dancers the b-boys."

Despite their age, Keith and Kevin soon established themselves as premier performers at Herc's parties. "When we danced, we always had a crowd around us," said Keith. "We wore Pro-Keds, double-knit pants, windbreakers, and hats we called 'crushers.' One of us would always have the hat on backwards and we both had straws in our mouth." During the week, the twins spent hours working on new routines, inventing steps that would amaze the crowd. "James Brown had a lot to do with it," explained Kevin, "because he used to do splits and slide across the floor."

Herc's partner was a 17-year-old weed dealer named Coke La Rock, a name lifted from a dream he had one night shortly after the parties got started. His nickname had been "Coco" because he loved chocolate milk as a child but that name was not considered cool or manly enough until he shortened it and added "La Rock." Selling drugs on the street was so common Coke assumed it was legal at the time. He would take over the turntables whenever

Herc needed a break and began rapping on the mic, which is how he became the first rapper in hip hop history. "You rock and you don't stop," was one of his favorite lines. He also invented: "Hotel, motel, you don't tell, we won't tell," and other lines that became South Bronx classics. Besides being the back-up deejay and first rapper, Coke also worked security and carried a gun, which was a good idea since he was usually carrying a few thousand dollars in weed profits and sold continuously during the parties.

The flyers for these parties were usually done by an artist named Funky Word. Herc insisted on the slogan printed at the bottom: "You've been entertained by the rest, now be entertained by the best: Kool DJ Herc and Coke La Rock, where you get the serious of the seri-o-so jointski's.

"Ski" was also a big phrase at the time, stuck on the end of proper names, like Soulski. A joint could be anything good, so I imagine a jointski meant better than your average joint (in this case "joint" meaning "record). I often wonder if this love of the word "joint" developed out of marijuana use, which was certainly widespread within the origins of the subculture (especially since cocaine and angel dust had not yet become popular—although both would soon have their own phases).

A couple of well-known stick-up kids began showing up, and especially feared was one named Frank Nitti, who robbed attendees and stayed at the party to continue a reign of terror all night long. One night 30 people were robbed. "We had to tell them to stop going to the bathroom," recalls Coke, "'cause they'd go in and come out naked. We couldn't protect that. We didn't search people. Everyone had guns."

In 1975, Herc moved into a club on 180th and Jerome Avenue. Formerly known as Soulsville, it had just been renamed the

Hevalo. With the gang situation cooling off, discos were just starting to reopen. Everybody wanted to get into dancing again. But while most deejays played the same disco hits one heard on the radio, the music at the Hevalo was harder, funkier. Herc knew how to bring the crowd up to a frenzied peak and hold them there for hours. During these times, he seldom played an entire song. Instead, he played the hottest segment of the song, which was often just a 30-second "break" section—when the drums, bass and rhythm guitar stripped the beat to its barest essence. Herc played break after break to create an endless peak of dance beats.

It wasn't long before the dancers at the Hevalo were known as "break" dancers. Rather than doing the Hustle or other disco steps, which required a male and female partner, break dancers usually performed solo. The dances evolved into a competition to establish who had the suavest, most graceful moves. The first break dancer was Sa-Sa. "He was a cat nobody could touch," recalls Coke. "He was double-jointed in his knees, which is how he came up with his drop."

"Before we called it 'breaking,' it was known as 'going off' or 'burning,'" said Phase. "When we were kids we did dances like the Washing Machine, the Popcorn, and the Mod Squad. The Busstop came out in 1974. Burning came out before the Busstop. It was all about taking a guy out, burning him. The big phrase was 'I'm gonna turn this party out.' I used to do shit with my feet that people didn't understand. I danced with three guys, Stak, Timbo and Sweet Duke. I think we brought a lot of shit out. This girl asked us: 'Where y'all learn to dance? You don't dance like nobody else.' Hand movements were really important, especially in a dance called the Salute. But I have to give credit to the Nigger Twins. Those boys were bad."

The free-lance deejay, an independent entrepreneur armed with a portable sound system and extensive record collection, emerged as the new cultural hero in the Bronx around 1975. Previously, anyone wishing to gain notoriety either became a graffiti writer or an incomparable break dancer. However, by 1976, the most powerful, most revered figures were the deejays. Herc remained in a class by himself, primarily because of his Macintosh amplifier and twin Shure speaker columns, the combination he called "The Herculords." The awesome power of the Herculords was most evident whenever Herc played the parks. Even outdoors, the system was surprisingly clean, free of distortion, and ear-shatteringly loud.

Herc also had the best records. While most other deejays played disco (Donna Summer and the Bee Gees were popular), Herc played hard-core funk with stripped-down drum beats. No record better epitomizes his style than *Apache*, a song recorded by the Ventures in the early sixties and redone by The Incredible Bongo Band in 1974. *Apache* combined a melodramatic, Spaghetti-Western melody with wild bongo solos, creating a theatrical atmosphere perfect for a showdown between two break dancers. Since it was recorded by an obscure record company, *Apache* was not an easy record to find. To make matters even more difficult, Herc jealously guarded the names of the most obscure break records, usually by painting over the labels or soaking them in his bathtub to remove the labels.

Other deejays began following Herc's style. At Stevenson High, Afrika Bambaataa formed a small group called the Zulus, who became an extension of the b-boy style, a gang into music and dance instead of violence. It wasn't long before the Zulus became a powerful force at Stevenson, so powerful, in fact, that the principal had Bambaataa transferred to a different school. On November 12, 1976, Bambaataa gave his first official party as a deejay at the Bronx Community Center.

Grandmaster Flash (center) and his crew before disharmony and cocaine abuse set in. "Sylvia," said Flash, "What is publishing?" That question got him fired, dragged into court, and took five years off his career.

At the time there were four main deejays playing "b-beat" music in the Bronx: Bambaataa in the southeast, Herc in the west, and, in the middle, an ambitious young deejay named Grandmaster Flash. Also of particular note was a deejay named Casanova Fly, who had developed a huge following in the South Bronx. Casanova could do it all, rap, draw, deejay, break dance. He was the original one-man hip hop show. After a deejay battle in which he took his skills to a new level, Fly became known as Grandmaster Caz. The other deejay who rose to early fame was Breakout, who formed the Funky Four + 1. However, there were also dozens of lesser-known deejays, all struggling for recognition. The easiest and quickest way to establish a reputation as a deejay was to "battle" a known deejay. These battles were usually held in parks or community centers. Both deejays played at the same time. Whoever collected the most dancers around his system was declared the winner. However, with both systems cranked to maximum volume, the winner was often the deejay with the loudest sound. "There was a lot of confusion going on at the time," laughed Bambaataa. "If you out-blasted the other deejay, he'd get mad, cut off his system and leave."

During one legendary battle against Disco King Mario, Bambaataa opened his show with the theme song from the Andy Griffith Show, taped off his television set. He mixed the ditty with a rocking drum beat, followed it with the Munsters' theme song, and quickly changed gears with *I Got the Feeling* by James Brown. His knack for coming up with unexpected cuts and "bugging out" the audience earned him the title "Master of Records."

During the summer of 1976, young b-boys cruised through the Bronx on bicycles, looking for block parties. "Where they jamming?" they'd ask anyone in the street. "Flash is jamming at Twenty-Three Park!" would come the reply, and before long several hundred kids, many of them stoned on marijuana or beer, would come pouring into the park where Joseph Sadler and Gene Livingston had their system wired to the base of a streetlight. The audience knew the two deejays only by their stage names: Grandmaster Flash and Mean Gene.

Flash, an electronics wizard from Samuel Gompers Vocational School, had been deejaying house parties for two years. In 1976, he began attracting widespread attention for his outdoor parties, which were usually held in a park at 169th Street and Boston Road.

"You had to be entertaining to throw block parties," said Flash. "It was always a rough crowd and there was never any security. If the crowd wasn't entertained, the situation could get very dangerous. I would go to the Hevalo sometimes to check Herc out, but Herc used to embarrass me quite a bit. He'd say 'Grandmaster Flash in the house,' over the mike, and then he'd cut off the highs and lows on his system and just play the mid-range. 'Flash,' he'd say, 'in order to be a qualified disc jockey, there is one thing you must have...highs.' Then Herc would crank up his highs and the high hat would be sizzling. 'And most of all, Flash,' he'd say, 'you must have...bass.' Well, when Herc's bass came in the whole place would be shaking. I'd get so embarrassed that I'd have to leave. My system couldn't compare."

However, if Flash couldn't compete with Herc's system, he was determined to find another way to establish himself as the premier deejay in the Bronx. He began visiting Manhattan discos, where deejays like Pete Jones were playing music for an older, more sophisticated audience. Although he disliked the music, Flash noticed that Jones knew more about mixing records than Herc. "It wasn't no hit-or-miss thing," said Flash. "Herc would drop the needle and cut the record in and hope he was in the right spot, but Pete knew how to pre-cue his records."

One night Jones relented and let Flash temporarily take over the controls of his system. "Once I put on the headphones, I knew the secret," said Flash. "A simple toggle switch let me hear what was on each turntable. At school, we called it a SPDT—single pole, double throw—switch. I didn't have one on my mixer, so I took some crazy glue and glued on on. I ran wires to my turntables and to a small amp, just powerful enough to drive a set of headphones. When Gene came back I told him: 'Gene, I got something here! I found a way to lock these beats up and keep the shit going!'"

Although Herc was the first deejay to buy two copies of the same record so that he could keep repeating the same break indefinitely, it was Flash who devised the method for repeating break sections while keeping a steady beat. Rather than find the section by chance, Flash began pre-cuing through headphones. He spent hours sitting in his room practicing his mixing technique. By playing short, rapid-fire cuts from a variety of records, he invented the art of musical collage. "Mean Gene never seemed to get the hang of it," said Flash, "but his baby brother, Theodore, used to skip school and hang out with me. That's when I discovered the clock theory and Theodore caught on to it right away." In order to make a mix using five or six different records, Flash had to be able to locate precise moments on each record in a matter of seconds. The problem was that every groove looked pretty much the same. How could you find the right spot fast enough? The solution, Flash discovered, was to "read" the record like a clock, using the record label as the dial.

Flyer by Buddy Esquire.

Ray Chandler, an independent concert promoter, approached Flash in 1976 and tried to convince him to open a regular nightspot. Because most of his fans were junior-high-school age, Flash was dubious. Why pay to see him when lots of other deejays were playing the parks for free? However, after Chandler found a tiny club on Boston Road, Flash agreed to give it a try. The club didn't have a name, but the front door was painted black, so they called it The Black Door.

"It had two rooms with a long hallway between them," said Flash. "Each room was about the size of a living room. First thing we did was have a lot of flyers made up. Phase and Buddy Esquire were the main flyer makers. Those guys were great. Chandler hired a crew to pass the flyers out at schools. We'd open at eleven o'clock and by midnight, the place was so packed you couldn't buy your way in. The doors wouldn't open back up until six or seven in the morning."

By this time, Flash had converted several members of his crew into "emcees," who were supposed to keep the crowd dancing by talking over a microphone. Most of the attention, however, was still centered on the dancers. "Everybody was doing the Freak," said Flash. "That was a dance that made it permissible for the male to damn near have sexual intercourse with the female. It was a fast dance and you would bounce around with the girl jammed against you. And she'd be doing it right back to you. With some girls, it was even permissible to have a guy in the front and one in back, like a sandwich! If you weren't on the dance floor when that shit was jumping off, you missed out. It got super frantic. I would blow my tweeters and they'd sound like gunshots. You think that would disturb the dancers? Hell no. I had to program a calm hour after the frantic hour just to bring the crowd back to a normal state of mind. Lots of stick-up kids were coming to the club and they were the type to go up to somebody and demand his gold chain. If you weren't ready to fight, you'd have to hand it over. There was this one record—*Listen to Me* by Baby Huey. Something happened every time I played it. We called it 'the trouble record.' The stick-up kids would start looking for somebody the minute they heard it. We were having problems until Chandler hired a former division of the Black Spades to act as security. They had changed their names to the Casanova Crew and we didn't have any more problems after the Casanovas started taking care of security."

Flyer by Phase 2.

Within a few months, Flash's popularity was soaring and he had to move to a bigger club. Despite his success, he continued improving and updating his technique. In 1977 he invented back-spinning, which allowed him to repeat phrases and beats from a record by rapidly spinning it backwards. For example, he would take a phrase like "Let's dance" and repeat it seven or eight times—without losing the beat. "We conquered quite a bit of territory," said Flash. "High-school kids were getting into the music and we knocked off all the high schools. But the pinnacle of our dream was to play the Audubon Ballroom."

Meanwhile, Theodore and his brother Gene had formed their own deejay crew with "Grand Wizard" Theodore as the star. Although only 13 at the time, Theodore was one of the few deejays who could compete with Flash. While Flash was perfecting the backspin, Theodore was working on a technical innovation of his own, an innovation he debuted at the Third Avenue Ballroom in 1978.

While practicing at home, Theodore noticed he could create sound effects by shifting the needle back and forth while keeping it in the groove. It wasn't always a pleasant sound—in fact, it could be highly irritating—but if controlled properly, it could also be explosively percussive. Many deejays were already familiar with the sound because they heard it in their earphones every time they pre-cued a record. Theodore wanted to try the sound in public, but he wasn't sure how the audience would react. "The Third Avenue Ballroom was packed," said Theodore, "and I figured I might as well give it a try. So, I put on two copies of *Sex Machine* and started scratching up one. The crowd loved it...they went wild."

"Scratching" was soon imitated and improved by other deejays, including Flash, Breakout, A.J., Jazzy Jay, and Charlie Chase. In a few years, Whiz Kid and Grandmaster DST would use the technique to create unbelievably smooth, synthesizer-like effects. However, in 1978, the focus began shifting away from the deejays and onto their emcees, who were busy creating a new, aggressive style of rapping on the mike. Before long, few kids wanted to be deejays anymore. Instead, they all wanted to be rappers.

Chapter 4: A New Rap Language

It was a hot, sweltering night in the Bronx, but waves of thunderclouds were gathering over Westchester County and it looked as though rain might be arriving to cool off the city. Although the rain never came, a lightning storm did, and at 8:30 P.M. several bolts struck the power transmission lines at Indian Point nuclear power plant, causing a short circuit. Like falling dominoes, relay circuits stretching south into the city began shutting off. Lights went blank, elevators stopped, subway cars rolled to a halt. Within 20 minutes it became the worst blackout since November 1965.

Grandmaster Caz at home, photo by Andre Grossmann, 1983.

Unlike the previous blackout, however, which had been remarkably trouble-free, the blackout of July 14, 1977, was almost immediately marred by reports of looting, arson and robbery, most of which came from the ghetto areas of Bedford-Stuyvesant, Brownsville, Harlem, and the South Bronx. By 10 o'clock, gangs of youths were congregating in front of the major stores. "Let's do it, let's do it," they'd say, trying to work up the nerve to break a window. A steel door guarding the Ace Pontiac Showroom on Jerome Avenue was smashed and 50 cars were driven off the lot. When police answered an emergency call from a supermarket on 138th Street they were bombarded by bricks and bottles. "They couldn't understand why we were arresting them," said Officer Gary Parlefsky of the 30th Precinct to a New York Times reporter. "They were angry with us. They said: 'I'm on welfare. I'm taking what I need. Why are you bothering me?'" Fires, many undoubtedly set by arsonists, illuminated the streets, which were lined with looters carrying TV sets, stereos, groceries, clothing, and anything else they could cart away. Within 24 hours, more than 3,000 people were arrested and 100 policemen were injured. The state troopers were rushed in to restore order. "The blackout just totaled the whole damn neighborhood," said Phase 2. "The businesses never came up out of it."

Until the blackout, few people realized the extent of the anger and frustration in the South Bronx, emotions that had been subdued but not eliminated by social programs like welfare, methadone treatment, and food stamps. It is not surprising that these hostile feelings were also reflected in the new style of rapping formulated during that same summer. Although it is difficult to trace the origins of rap, the genre is firmly embedded in black American culture and stretches back farther than even most rappers realize.

In 1976, Dennis Wepman, Ronald Newman, and Murray Binderman published a landmark study on black prison culture entitled The Life: The Lore and Folk Poetry of the Black Hustler.

The book documented "toasting," a form of poetic storytelling prevalent in prisons throughout the fifties and sixties. "Toasts are a form of poetry recited by certain blacks—really a performance medium," wrote the authors. "They are like jokes: no one knows who creates them, and everyone has his own versions....Most recitation sessions are somewhat structured: a reciter performs to a silent, appreciative audience. Good tellers may be highly valued and much in demand....In Attica, Doe Eye, a young burglar from Harlem, could characterize the people of the toasts so exactly that, when he was speaking from his cell, one might have thought he had a group in there with him."

Probably the oldest and most famous toast, "The Signifying Monkee," had hundreds of different versions by 1976. Other famous toasts included "Duriella du Fontaine" and "King Heroin," a version of which was recorded by James Brown in 1972. Some toasts were moralistic fables, others related how a man in prison had been betrayed by a girl friend. Almost all attempted to glorify the life of the petty criminal. The toast that follows was probably composed in 1964.

THE HUSTLER

The name of the game is beat the lame
Take a woman amd make her line in shame.
It makes no difference how she scream or holler,
'Cause dope is my heaven and my God the almighty dollar.
I, the Hustler, swear by God
I would kill Pope Paul if pressed too hard.
I would squash out Bobby and do Jackie harm
And for one goddamn dollar
would break her arm.
I, the Hustler, kick ass morning, noon and night.
I would challenge Cassius and Liston to a fight.
I would climb in the ring

> *with nothing but two P-38s.*
> *And send either one that moved*
> *through the pearly gates.*
> *I, the Hustler, can make Astaire dance*
> *and Sinatra croon,*
> *And I would make the Supreme Court eat shit from a spoon.*

During the fifties, black radio jocks entertained and amused audiences with prison-style raps. In 1955, the most popular of these radio personalities was Douglas "Jocko" Henderson, whose "1280 Rocket" show on WOV anticipated a hip hop fascination with themes from outer space. Jocko often opened his show with lines like: "From way up here in the stratosphere, we gotta holler mighty loud and clear 'ee-tiddy-o and a ho," and I'm back on the scene with the record machine, saying 'oo-pap-doo' and how do you do!" His witty, bantering style was updated and refined by New York club deejays like Frankie Crocker, who later became a radio jock on WBLS.

It is worth noting that Jamaican music also has a history of toasting: poems written in Jamaican slang were spoken to the beat of reggae records by deejays with enormous portable sound systems. Because of this, many critics have drawn parallels between the development of rap and reggae, a connection that is denied by Kool Herc. "Jamaican toasting?" said Herc. "Naw, naw. No connection there. I couldn't play reggae in the Bronx. People wouldn't accept it. The inspiration for rap is James Brown and the album Hustler's Convention."

Released in 1973, Hustler's Convention was written and performed by Jalal Uridin, leader of a group of black militant ex-cons known as the Last Poets. The group was discovered in the late sixties by record producer Alan Douglas, who saw them on a local television show. "I called the station, found out who it was, and though some sources I made a contact. I went to 138th Street and Lenox Avenue one afternoon and they recited for me on the street corner," said Douglas. "I made a deal with them. The deal was, they would come to the recording studio, put this on tape, and if we all like each other when it was over, I'd put the record out. And if they didn't, they could take the master home with them."

The group's first record, which contained such raps as "Run Nigger," "Niggers Are Scared of Revolution," and "When the Revolution Comes," reportedly sold more than 800,000 copies despite its aggressively radical overtones, which annihilated any hope of radio play. Under the pseudonym "Lightin' Rod," Jalal went on to record Hustler's Convention, a solo album also produced by Douglas. It consisted of twelve prison toasts (with raps like "Four Bitches is What I Got," "Coppin' Some Fronts for the Set," and "Sentenced to the Chair") recited to musical compositions by Brother Gene Dinwiddie and Kool & The Gang. Although the record did not sell as well as Jalal's initial effort, it had enormous popularity in the Bronx.

With Hustler's Convention as inspiration, Kool Herc and Coke La Rock began composing prison-style rhymes using expressions like "my mellow" and "it's the joint." Herc discovered an echo chamber could provide dramatic flourishes at just the right moments. "Yes, yes, y'all," Herc would say. "It's the serious, serio-so jointski. You're listening to the sound system. The Herculords...culords...lords. And I just want to say to all my b-boys...boys...oys. Rock on. Time to get down to the AM. But please remember—respect my system and I'll respect you and yours. As I scan the place, I see the very familiar face...of my mellow. Wallace Dee in the house. Wallace Dee, freak for me."

"I first went to the Hevalo with I was thirteen," said Sisco Kid. "This dude around my block said, 'Hang with me,' and he took me. Everybody was lined up around the block. They had a gangster look and were older than me. I said, 'Oh shit, this is crazy.' It was very dark inside, but there was an excitement in the air, like anything could jump off. You'd see some dude dancing and he'd be wearing alligator shoes. You'd say, 'Check out this dude!' Then Herc came on the mike and he was so tough. You'd get transfixed by his shit. He had this def voice that almost sounded like a southern drawl. You thought, 'This is cool, I want to be like this.'"

"People got ideas from Hustler's Convention," said Theodore. "But it was hard to get on the mike and say a rhyme. Noboby really had any rhymes. Mostly it was 'You're listening to the sound of so-and-so deejay and next week we'll be at such-and-such park.' Then Flash wrote this rhyme. 'You dip, dive and socialize. We're trying to make you realize. That we are qualified to rectify that burning...desire..to boogie.' At this point he didn't have any emcees. He asked Melle Mel, 'Will you say this rhyme?' Mel said, 'No, let Cowboy say it.' Cowboy said, 'No, let Mel say it.' It went back and forth like that. Flash wanted that rhyme said so bad he finally grabbed the mike and said, 'I'll say it.' And that's how it happened."

Vocal entertainment became necessary to keep the crowd under control," said Flash. "When people first came to the park, they'd start dancing. But then everyone would gather around and watch the deejay. A block party could turn into a seminar. That was dangerous. You needed vocal entertainment to keep everyone dancing. I tried so many people. I used to leave the mike on the other side of the table so anybody who wanted could pick it up. A lot of people failed the test. The first to pass was Cowboy. Then Mel. Then Mel's brother Creole."

Since Cowboy had a deep voice similar to that of a radio disk jockey, his early rapping style more closely emulated disco deejays like Hollywood, a Manhattan-based deejay who employed a slick, radio-jock sound. Mel and Creole, on the other hand, created a more percussive style of rap similar to the staccato exhortations used by James Brown on such hip hop classics as "Give It Up or Turn It Loose," a song in which key phrases were shouted to the beat. "Clap your hands!" screamed Brown. "Stomp your feet! In the jungle, brother! Clap! Clap! Ain't it funky now? Need to feel it!" Although Brown's vocals could not really be called rap, they provided the perfect accompaniment for dance records: They encouraged the audience to participate more fully in the music, they emphasized rhythm and raw emotion over melody, and each syllable was spoken directly on the beat— something that had not been attempted with toasting, which put its emphasis on vocal ingenuity and lyrical content rather than rhythm. (Douglas attributes the difference to a change in musical styles. "The Last Poets were jazz heads," he explained, "while today's rappers are into disco, rock and rhythm & blues. The words fall differently and you get a different feeling. The Poets didn't care if one could dance to the rap. The point was a story was going down that was memorable.")

Relying on an inventive use of slang, the percussive effect of short words, and unexpected internal rhymes, Mel and Creole began composing elaborate rap routines, intricately weaving their voices through a musical track mixed by Flash. They would trade solos, chant, and sing harmony. The result was dazzling. It was a vocal style that effectively merged the aggressive rhythms of James Brown with the language and imagery of Hustler's Convention. They were immediately imitated by every other emcee in the Bronx.

> *To the hip hop, hip hop, don't stop*
> *Don't stop that body rock.*
> *Just get with the beat, get ready to clap.*
> *'Cause Melle Mel, is starting to rap*
> *Ever since the time of the very first party.*
> *I felt I could make myself some money.*

> *It was up in my heart from the very start.*
> *I could super sell, at the top of the charts.*
> *Rappin' on the mike, makin' cold cold cash.*
> *With a jock spinnin' for me called deejay Flash.*

To complement the new rap routines, Flash experimented with a recently invented electronic percussion machine. The shock value alone made the machine a useful theatrical device. The turntables would be empty, Flash would step back from his set, and yet somehow the beats would continue with mechanical precision. "It bugged them out," said Flash, laughing. "Then we started featuring ourselves as Grandmaster Flash and the Three Emcees...with THE BEAT BOX. People would show up at the party just to see what the beat box was."

The rap style pioneered by Coke La Rock and Cowboy was taken to new levels by the Funky Four, who had a secret weapon: the first female rapper, a girl named Sha-Rock. Sha-rock took the usual trajectory to reach this position: she started as a b-girl. Everybody immediately knew who the b-boys were in the Bronx because they had a new style and tons of attitude. Sha-rock convinced a friendly b-boy to show her some of his power moves. Before long, Sha-Rock could break dance just like the boys and quickly moved to master the art of rapping. She eventually wrote a wonderful autobiography that describes her audition for Breakout's new group. It was her first experience with marijuana, although she acted a veteran. She blew away the competition and was inducted on the spot. The Funky Four quickly became the first rap group to perform with mike stands and develop elaborate dancing routines. Suddenly, they were on top of rap world.

Meanwhile, failing to keep up with recent developments in deejay skills, Kool Herc was having trouble maintaining his position, and, in fact, was undergoing a rapid decline in popularity, a development he attributed to being stabbed at one of his own parties. "The party hadn't even started," said Herc. "Three guys came to the door and my people wouldn't let them in. They said they was looking for the owner. A discrepancy started. By this time, I'm finished dressing and I walk over and say, "What's happening?' Boom, boom, boom. I got stabbed three times, once in the hand and twice in the side. The guy with the knife was drunk. I took a piece of ice, put it on my side, and walked to the hospital."

Coke had gone home for a few minutes and when he came back and found Herc had gone to the hospital, he became frantic looking for the perpetrator, who he certainly planned to shoot dead on sight. That plan was thwarted, however, when friends moved perpetrator down south for a few months just to avoid a confrontation with the enraged Coke La Rock. But the incident spelled the beginning of the end for Coke, because he'd just had a child and the thought of going to jail for murder didn't seem very appealing, although he felt compelled to follow through with street justice because security had been his job and Herc was his best friend. Slowly, Coke and Herc began fading from the scene.

For over two years rap had developed in almost complete isolation from the rest of the world. Until 1980, hip hop music and rap were transmitted primarily through live cassette recordings that were noisily displayed via ghetto blasters, portable tape machines carried by every self-respecting hip hopper. Tapes were circulated around New York, in prisons, in nearby states, and could even be found on army bases overseas. However, the first rap record using the South Bronx style was made not by a local group but by the Fatback Band, who recorded "King Tim II" in 1979. Several months later, Sylvia Robinson, a former singer who recorded "Pillow Talk" and "Love is Strange" in the 1970s, decided to make a rap record. One day she walked into a pizza shop near her home in New Jersey and heard a live tape being played by a man named Hank, who was the doorman at a rap club in the Bronx.

The tape featured Grandmaster Caz and the Mighty Force Emcees.

"The way rap evolved is from people trying to outdo each other," said Grandmaster Caz. "You'd go to Herc's party and hear him say something. Then you'd go home and change it around to where it was your saying. I knew the entire Hustler's Convention by heart. That was rap, but we didn't know it at the time. Then everybody started saying nursery rhymes. Then Flash started the whole thing of having real groups. Then people started coming to parties just to see the emcees. I used to go to this club called the Sparkle and I told Hank about my group. I told him we needed a manager. So he went to work for us, helping us out on the financial ends and stuff. He was also working at the pizza shop and that's where he met Sylvia. She heard him playing one of our tapes. So he told me about it. Later, I asked him, 'Whatsup?' and he said, 'Sylvia already has two rappers and she wants one more. And she asked me to do it.' So I said, 'Well, okay, I understand that.' If it was me, I would have done the same thing. And he said, 'Well, I want to use some of your rhymes.' I threw my rhyme book on the table and said, 'Take what you want.'"

Before long Robinson created the Sugarhill Gang, a group composed of Hank, Wonder Mike, and Master Gee. Their first record, "Rapper's Delight," unexpectedly sold two million copies, launched a new independent record company, and created a vast audience for rap music around the country. It also unleashed a mad scramble of emcee groups looking for record contracts. The song's success was due more to its novelty and its musical track, which was lifted from Chic's "Good Times," than to its rapping, which was weak and unimaginative by Bronx standards.

"I never thought about how big it might come out," said Caz. "I never thought Hank would become a millionaire and forget about me. When the record came out, I was going to high school at

Roosevelt and every car that passed had it on the radio. Every box on the street had it on. Everybody knew those rhymes were mine and half were coming up to me, 'Yo, I heard you on the radio!' The other half was saying, 'You're not gettin' no money for that!' I never saw Hank again. It was like he was afraid to approach me."

(Caz later joined the Cold Crush Brothers and signed a contract with Tuff City, a subsidiary of CBS.)

When emcee groups realized they were the primary reason why many people were coming to hip hop parties, they demanded more money from their deejays, which led to arguments and eventual breakups. At the time, Bambaataa was working with a number of groups, including Soul Sonic Force, Cosmic Force, and the Jazzy Five. However, he freely admits the most "treacherous" battles were taking place between Flash and the Furious Five versus Breakout and the Funky Four. "Flash was on top," said Bambaataa, "but they was battling for that number-one spot. Both groups was doin' flips on stage and settin' off smoke bombs." Theodore and his brother Gene formed a group called the L-Brothers, later known as the Fantastic Freaks. "Waterbed" Kev, one of their rappers, began wearing studded belts and chains, a style soon imitated by almost every other group. (Within three years, this "S&M look" would be picked up by thousands of teenagers around the city.)

In 1979, Special K, a Bronx rapper and member of the Undefeated Four, was attending Townes High School on 33rd Street in Manhattan. "I was not known as just a rapper," said Special K, "I was known as a Bronx rapper 'cause Manhattan rappers had more of a disco style with much more slang. My brother used to go to Stevenson High and he knew Breakout and Bambaataa. He was a break dancer —a member of the Zulu Masters. When rap came out, it wasn't about having a record deal or doing shows, it was about writing rhymes. It was a habit. I would write while walking down the hallway at school. At Townes I met the Treacherous Three, which was Spoonie Gee, L.A. Sunshine and Kool Mo Dee. One time they invited me to come down to one of their parties. First we was having battles, but then they started talking about getting together. I considered it and went back to the Bronx. Then, I found out Spoonie Gee had made a record, so I said, 'Ohh no, let me shoot on back down and see whatsup.'"

"'Rapper's Delight' changed everything," said Kool Mo Dee. "Spoonie's uncle Bobby Robinson [no relation to Sylvia Robinson] had a little record company called Enjoy, and Spoonie wanted to make a record. At first his uncle didn't pay him no mind, but after 'Rapper's Delight' came out, Spoonie's uncle got interested. He asked Spoonie who the best rappers were and Spoonie said the Funky Four and Flash. Then Spoonie made a record where he talked about how good he was in bed. That was his gimmick. Everybody had a gimmick. L.A. Sunshine's gimmick was his voice sounded like Hollywood, so we called him Baby Hollywood. My gimmick was using big words like 'establishment,' 'repent,' stuff like that. Spoonie had a whole book of rhymes on different ways to have sex. He got a lot of attention 'cause the girls like to hear that stuff. We asked Spoonie, 'Why didn't you take us down to the studio with you?' He said, 'I didn't think it was no big thing.' So Spoonie started doing shows by himself, only sometimes he'd get lonely and ask me to come with him. Spoonie had an ego at that time 'cause he had the most juice from his record. During that summer I made up fast rapping, a new style of talking very fast. We got to make a record with Spoonie as the Treacherous Three. That's when Special K became a member of the group."

The records sold better than Robinson expected, and it wasn't long before Grandmaster Flash, the Funky Four, and Spoonie Gee were lured away to the more successful Sugarhill label, leaving Robinson with the Treacherous Three. "We had a good relationship with Bobby," said Mo Dee. "He was very funny. The money as comin' in fast. We would never get checks, but when we saw Bobby he would feed us money. We was getting a lot of attention." "Yeah, but he flaked when it came to royalties," added Special K. "We made three more records on Enjoy and then Bobby sold us to Sugarhill."

During the spring of 1981, the Treacherous Three released two records in rapid succession: "The Body Rock" and "Put the Boogie in the Body." The former featured a peppy, well-coordinated rap routine, a slow, slinky beat dominated by a synthesizer bass line, and some shrieking, post-psychedelic guitar riffs. It was an infectious dance record and became an instant street classic. Even more effective, however, was the group's next release, "Put the Boogie in the Body," which remains one of the highest-energy raps every recorded. After opening with a series of shouts, the song builds in intensity for six minutes before ending in a fade-out of garbled nonsense words. Since the instrumental track is spare and minimal, the emotional force of this song is carried entirely by the rappers. Shortly before the record's release, The Treacherous Three established themselves as one of the premier rap groups in the city.

"A lot of people thought rap was going to fade out," said Special K. "They thought it was a fad and looked at rappers as being unintelligent, high-school dropouts. But it seemed like every time rap got ready to die, something new came along to add a new dimension—to boost it along."

Chapter 5: But Is It Art?

Moody, intense, often uncommunicative, Lee Quinones was never mistaken for just another graffiti writer. A short Puerto Rican with a prominent scar across the bridge of his nose, Quinones usually wore a car mechanic's overalls with a Plymouth insignia sewn over the breast pocket. In 1975, when he snuck into a subway yard to paint his first whole-car mural, half of the car was dominated by a large, brightly colored "LEE" outline, the obligatory element in every graffiti masterpiece, but the other half portrayed two derelicts standing in front of a burning building. Instead of "throwing-up" large numbers of quickly executed pieces, Quinones concentrated exclusively on well-painted, whole-car murals. When it came to graffiti, he seemed zealous, resolute, and driven by forces he could not express through any means except his paintings.

Although the graffiti subculture had quieted down after the breakup of UGA, it reached a new peak of activity during 1976, when whole-car murals began appearing in ever-increasing numbers. Because of his growing reputation, Quinones was approached by four writers interested in forming a new group called the Fabulous Five (formerly the name of a Manhattan streetgang). "Slug was the leader," said Quinones. "He used to be a Black Spade and we was very smart, very philosophical. The others were Doc and Mono, who had been members of a gang called The Puerto Rican Brothers, and Slave, who was a tall, skinny writer from Brooklyn." The Fabulous Five quickly established themsevles as the premier writing group in the city. They robbed paint stores, drank beer, stayed up unti dawn, and spent endless weeks doing nothing but painting trains. One winter they pulled off the ultimate graffiti masterpiece—a ten car train with a mural on every car. However, in the world of subway graffiti, kings are easily deposed. Each year a new generation of writers appears and the younger ones tend to be more ambitious and energetic than their older counterparts, who move into more profitable, less dangerous occupations. By 1978, Quinones was the only member of the Fabulous Five still painting graffiti.

Lee Quinones in the film Wild Style.

Many writers dropped out in 1977, when the Transit Authority erected its "final solution" to the graffiti problem in a Coney Island train yard. At an annual cost of $400,000, the T.A. began operating a giant carwash that sprayed vast amounts of petroleum hydroxide on the sides of graffitied trains. The solvent spray was followed by a vigorous buffing. At first the writers called it "the Orange Crush," after Agent Orange, a defoliant used in Vietnam. Later it was simply known as "the buff." Fumes emanating from the cleaning station were so deadly that a nearby school closed after students complained of respiratory problems. The school later reopened after city officials assured the community that the health complaints had nothing to do with the graffiti removal operation. However, even T.A. workers admitted they couldn't stand downwind from the station without getting nauseous. Meanwhile, the solvent was seeping into the underfloorings of the trains, causing considerable corrosion and damaging electrical parts.

A few writers were sure the buff meant the end of graffiti: Phase wrote a rap elegy titled "After the Buff," and Tracy designed a cartoon with the inscription "Graffiti R.I.P." However, the buff never really eliminated graffiti. Instead, it mixed the spray paint into a single grayish mudlike color. Writers soon learned to use better-quality paints and to spray murals with a protective covering of clear enamel. They couldn't defeat the buff entirely, but the T.A. had to run a train through the station several times before the murals were obliterated.

Quinones had a better solution. In 1979, he began painting handball courts around the Lower East Side. The concept of murals on handball courts had originated with Tracy several years earlier. However, Quinones was the first writer to become known primarily for painting them. Like his work on the trains, Quinones's court murals mingled cartoon imagery with a strong moral sensibility. One mural pleaded for an end to the arms race, while another portrayed a ten-foot-tall Howard the Duck (a character from Marvel Comics) emerging from a trash can, with the inscription: "If art like this is a crime, let God forgive me."

One day, while sitting in class at Seward High School, Quinones was approached by a tall black man wearing dark sunglasses. "I want to talk to you, man," said the stranger. Before he could say another word, the teacher removed him from the class. "When class was over, the dude was still waiting for me outside," said Quinones. "I was expecting a fight. But it turned out he just wanted to talk about what was happening on the trains. I didn't know if he was a policeman or what—so I gave him the brush-off." However, the man, whose name was Fred Brathwaite, kept returning to see Quinones. "He said he knew a way to make money with graffiti. I started thinking about what he was proposing and said, 'Well, let's give it a try.'"

A few weeks later, Brathwaite appeared with a clipping from the *Village Voice*. In the February 12, 1979, "Scenes" column was a photo of Brathwaite standing in front of one of Lee's murals. A brief article by Howard Smith followed.

"We call ourselves the Fabulous Five and we're the best at what we do—graffiti. Just recently we decided to start selling our services for $5 per square foot, and already we've got several commissions. All we need is for more folks to give us a chance. I mean, we're really incredible at redoing storefronts, old grimy walls, sides of trucks, boring bulding lobbies, interiors, exteriors. You name it; pay us; we'll paint it..."

"Are you kidding?" [Smith] interrupted. "Most people I know in the city are trying to get rid of you spray-can freaks."

Standing in front of me, his mouth open in shock, was Frederick Brathwaite, leader of the Fabulous Five. He puffed himself up in his spiffy suit and tie, and pounced back: "It's that kind of attitude I have to fight. I think it's time everyone realized graffiti is the purest form of New York art. What else has evolved from the streets? Lee, Doc, Slave, Mono and I are just taking it off the trains and bringin' it above ground...As you can see, we've obviously been influenced by Warhol, Crumb, and Lichtenstein..."

The article included a telephone number and address where Brathwaite could be reached for possible commissions.

Martinez may have been the first outsider to market graffiti, but he lacked a flair for the promotional intricacies of the art world. Brathwaite, on the other hand, was an insider to the subculture who realized the importance of connecting graffiti with the hip downtown art scene—especially Andy Warhol, an artist many writers had probably never heard of, much less used as an influence. "Fred knew it was about time for graffiti to get going again," saya Quinones.

Brathwaite received several calls after the article appeared, but the most important one came from Claudio Bruni, and Italian art dealer who maintained a New York residence. Bruni told Brathwaite he could arrange a show if he had some work on canvas. Brathwaite and Quinones immediately went to work. "Claudio came and bought five paintings outright," said Quinones. "At first, I wasn't really interested in the money. I just wanted to preserve my work. But the money started coming in after Claudio arranged a show in Rome. We flew over for the opening. They had a party and all the chic people came." Bruni had no trouble selling the work at $1,000 a canvas.

Brathwaite wasn't the only writer who sensed a graffiti might be making a commerical comeback. Mark Edmonds (Ali), who had miraculously recovered from his subway accident without a single facial scar, reformed Soul Artists after receiving a grant from an arts organization. Ali wrote a letter to Futura 2000, who had served out his enlistment and was living in Georgia with a Navy buddy, urging him to return to New York. Although Futura did return, several months passed before he would enter a subway yard. The two friends did not discuss the accident and their relationship remained somewhat strained.

Three other contacts with the legitimate art world took place during this period. Stefan Eins, an artist and gallery owner who was operating a gallery on Mercer Street in Soho, decided to move his business to the South Bronx. "I wanted a stronger challenge," explained Eins. "If you continue to show the artists you know, you wind up following the same direction in the same social climate. It was very sobering to be in the Bronx. I couldn't fall into any art world patterns." Through his new gallery, Fashion Moda, Eins began cultivationg a relationship with the local graffiti artists.

Sam Esses, a burly, outspoken collector from Park Avenue, became aware of a growing European interest in graffiti though conversations with the Italian dealer Bruni. When he discovered that his daughter knew some writers, he decided to make contact. "I don't know why, but I decided to rent a studio to see if I could preserve some of the work that was being created on the trains," said Esses. "I found an empty space on the Upper East Side and stocked it with supplies." Word soon spread through the graffiti grapevine, and the best writers from all over the city materialized on Esses's doorstep. Dozens of large canvases were completed and Esses set about finding a gallery to show the work. Although the exhibit was not held for two years, the "workshop" encouraged many writers to continue working on canvas.

A sculptor named Henry Chalfant, who had been taking pictures of graffiti for several years, decided to meet some writers. He visited the writer's bench at 149th Street and the Grand Concourse, where he showed his photos to several kids, who insisted on introducing Chalfant to Crash, a promising young writer and protege of Kase 2, the current style master of the Bronx. Around the same time, Chalfant approached Ivan Karp of O.K. Harris Gallery, who agreed to exhibit the photos in the fall.

During the summer of 1980, many observers of the art scene sensed something new was in the air. Although critics had been discussing the "death" of painting for almost a decade, the art market was booming, primarily due to the emergence of a cadre of upper-middle-class collectors, many of whom were looking for undiscovered artists to decorate the walls of their Upper East Side co-ops. Impoverished young painters denied access to the major galleries rushed to fill the demand. Minimalism, the foremost movement of the seventies, was exhausted, and it was obvious that a new "movement" was needed. The term "new wave" was coined to describe the connection between art and current developments in rock music. Another popular term, "neo-expressionism," described the return to recognizable imagery that was taking place simultaneously in several European countries as well as the United States.

In June, the young, aspiring artists and the graffiti writers got together for the first time in the Times Square Show, which opened in an abandoned massage parlor on 41st Street. The meeting proved extremely beneficial for both groups. Organized by Collaborative Projects (Colab), an independent, democratic collection of struggling young artists, the Times Square Show was a chaotic display of aggressive erotica, graffiti, "punk" art, and political manifestos. Stairways were strewn with broken glass, walls were splashed with paint, and life-size rat sculptures were placed strategically throughout the building's five floors in an effort to create a proper environment for the work of more than 150 sculptors, painters, photographers, filmmakers, and conceptual artists. Patrons of the local porno movie houses wandered in, as did prostitutes, pimps, winos, newspaper reporters, and art collectors. Samo, a conceptual graffiti artist, wrote "FREE SEX" over the doorway, a statement that was hastily painted over by one of the show's organizers. Keith Haring, a recent dropout from the School of Visual Arts (SVA), was among the many exhibitors inside.

Haring, who had a round, boyish face, closely cropped hair, a receding hairline, and small blue eyes, had been keeping an eye on subway graffiti since he moved to New York from Kutztown, Pennsylvania, in 1978. "The name 'Lee' really stuck out," he said. "I learned a lot about art by looking at his work." Although he had made a few tentative forays into graffiti art (composing William Burroughs-style "cut-ups" of fake newspaper headlines and posting them on the street, along with a few other short-lived projects), it wasn't until the Times Square Show that Haring met his first graffiti artist: Fred Brathwaite, who by that time had changed his name to Fab Five Freddy.

"Fred had two paintings in the show," said Haring. "But I didn't know who he was. I was standing next to him and I pointed at the paintings and said, 'This is Fab Five Freddy. He had a show in Italy.' Then I talked about graffiti. Fred said, "Uhuh,' like he didn't know what I was talking about. He had a sketch book in his hand and I asked to look at it. When I opened the book, I realized who he was and that I'd just put my foot in my mouth."

After the Times Square Show, Haring began producing the graffiti that eventually made him famous. When the city began covering unrenewed poster ads with black tar paper, he began drawing on this black paper with chalk. He developed an elaborate vocabulary of images that included crawling babies, barking dogs, space ships, telephones, TV sets, kand atomic explosions. The images were instantly recognizable yet seemed to be involved in a mysterious, indecipherable narrative.

"We'd be walking down the street and Keith would just stop and do a drawing," said his friend and fellow artist Kenny Scharf. "They took about three minutes. He was fanatical about it. There were chalk drawings everywhere. He did so many it was unbelievable. A big crowd would usually form around him. Some people would say nice things. Everybody knew his work."

Unlike most graffiti, Haring's work was almost universally admired. Although the drawings could be easily rubbed off, they were seldom touched. One of the early efforts, executed on the door of a Times Square newspaper stand, remained intact for two months before being covered by a handbill. "The power of graffiti tags is that they come straight out of the head and onto the wall," said Haring. "There's no turning back. You've got to be completely on while it's happening. The real thing is the act of doing it. It's really hard to achieve complete control with no inhibitions. You see it in Chinese calligraphy. All my drawings were done in one shot. Some people have the mistaken idea that I drew in the subway, saw that it worked, and then started doing work for the galleries. It didn't happen like that. I've always been drawing. The subways was just another place to put the work. And I didn't put anything in the streets until I'd looked at graffiti for several years. There's an unwritten code about what belongs in the street. It's a big responsibility, it's a big step to put your work there. In some ways, it's hard to argue whether you have the right, but at some point you make the decision, partly so that people who would otherwise never see the work will be confronted with it. When I arrived in New York, it was obvious the art world really had nothing to do with what was happening in the streets. It was off on its own intellectual tangent."

Haring began attending weekly meetings of the Soul Artists, which were held at Ali's house. He met Futura, Zephyr, SE3, Daze, and other S.A. members. At the time, Soul Artists meetings were drawing some of the more prominent writers around town, including Dondi, who led a group in Brooklyn known as the Crazy Inside Artists (CIA), and Quinones, who attended a few meetings without actually joining. An independent filmmaker named Charlie Ahearn showed up and announced his plans to direct a feature film on the subculture.

In December 1980, Richard Goldstein, author of the first pro-graffiti story in *New York* magazine back in 1973, wrote an extensive article on the new graffiti writers in the *Village Voice*. The article was especially important because it linked graffiti and rap music for the first time. "The big lie is that graffiti is confined to 'antisocial' elements," wrote Goldstein. "Increasingly, it is the best and the brightest who write on subway walls, tenement halls.

Unlike the newspaper that has called for their demise, these bands are racially integrated, which gives writers access to the same cross-cultural energy that animates rock 'n' roll. In fact, the graffiti sensibility has a musical equivalent in 'rap records'—another rigid, indecipherable form that can sustain great complexity."

Although Goldstein's awareness of rap music was probably limited (most of his readers undoubtedly didn't even know what the term meant), his assumption that rap sprang from the same cultural conditions as graffiti was certainly correct. Goldstein went on to discuss Haring, a completely unknown artist at the time, and several other artists who were currently being influenced by the graffiti esthetic, including Samo (now known as Jean-Michel Basquiat) and John Fekner. Even more important was the accompanying two-page photo spread in blazing color, showing six whole-car designs by Dondi, Lee, Blade, Seen, Futura, and Kell. Taken by Henry Chalfant, the photos introduced many New Yorkers to the glory of a freshly painted (and unbuffed) graffiti mural for the first time.

Just as new wave music inspired artists like Robert Longo and Laurie Anderson in the 1980 art season, the commercial success of rap music furthered graffiti art. Mention of the graffiti writers began appearing in the music press, and several prominent writers went on to record rap records, including Phase 2, Futura, and Brathwaite. When Kurtis Blow released "The Breaks," Futura went to the yards to pay homage to the record. The result was a full-car mural that looked like a relic from a nuclear holocaust. He painted the car to look blistered, as if it had been driven through a terrible fire. In the center he put a jagged hole big enough to drive a Volkswagen through. Since 1973, writers had been painting cracks in their letters, but Futura was the first to crack an entire car. A network of blue-and-violet circles appeared to drift across the car's surface, and, in contrast to these amorphous shapes, he added four constuctivist-style symbols. Goldstein accused him of imitating Kandinsky, an artist whose work Futura had never seen.

In February, a sprawling exhibit titled "New York/New Wave" opened at P.S. 1, an alternative space in Long Island City, Queens. Curated by Diego Cortez, it was the first attempt to document the crossover between art and music that had taken place during the previous two years. Drawings, photographs, and video works by such rock stars as David Byrne, Alan Vega, and Brian Eno were placed alongside documentary photographs taken at rock clubs and scores of neo-expressionist paintings by undiscovered artists. An entire wall was filled with massive murals by members of the Soul Artists. Many people came away feeling the graffiti writers had stolen the show.

Brathwaite, temporarily known as Freddy Love, became the unofficial spokesman for hip hop. A raconteur of considerable skill, he entertained reporters with stories about his early days in Brooklyn and educated them in the inner workings of the subculture, as well as his knowledge of the counterculture, including its birth in Congo Square, New Orleans, a heritage he'd learned from a famous uncle. Fred introduced the South Bronx scene to such downtown hipsters as Diego Cortez, rock critic Glenn O'Brien, and underground film star Patti Astor, who already had a reputation as the blonde bombshell of the Lower East Side. "I met Patti at a birthday party for Stephanie Marleme held at Duncan Smith's house," said Brathwaite. "I'd just seen her movie Underground USA and she was my favorite movie star. So I asked her for her autograph." Astor signed a scrap of paper and kissed it, leaving a perfect lipstick imprint.

A month later, when Haring was hired to operate a gallery space above the rock disco the Mudd Club, the Soul Artists were approached for an exhibit. Curated by Futura and Brathwaite, "Beyond Words" drew one of the largest and rowdiest art crowds of the season. Brathwaite arranged for Afrika Bambaataa to perform at the opening. It was his first contact with the hip downtown scene and Bambaataa was enormously impressed by the audience, especially when they gave his record "Zulu Nation Throwdown" an appreciative response. "I didn't even like the record that much," said Bambaataa, "but downtown everybody thought it was a classic. After that, I started liking it too."

Patti Astor, also in attendance at the exhibition, immediately fell in love with hip hop. An ex-revolutionary from the sixties and dropout from Barnard College, Astor had studied acting at the Lee Strasberg Institute before landing the leading role in Amos Poe's Unmade Beds, a $5,000, 16mm remake of Godard's Breathless, which was shot in 1976. "It was all very existential, I assure you," said Astor, laughing. "It was shown at the Deauville Film Festival and the cast flew over for the party, but I'm not sure the French got it." With her girlish, giggly voice, Jayne Mansfield figure, and classical face, Astor had no trouble landing roles in a slew of underground films like Rome '78, Long Island Four, and Underground USA. However, none achieved anything close to commercial success. When Astor discovered that her old friend Charlie Ahearn was making a film on hip hop titled Wild Style, she began pressuring him for a part.

In May, Astor and Ahearn bumped into each other at a rapper's convention in Harlem. "Patti was wearing a silver jumpsuit and she was probably the only white woman there," said Ahearn. "She was really throwing out her stardom vibes. People were staring at her like she was made of gold. I still wasn't sure I wanted her in the film. I was thinking it over. A week later I made up my mind. Of course, she turned out to be the perfect choice. The character she played in the film was the same character she was playing that night at the rap convention."

Astor was cast as a reporter who traveled to the South Bronx, discovered the graffiti scene, and brought it back to the established art world, a role she would eventually play in real life. During the filming, she supported herself by working for her friend Bill Stelling, who ran a roommate referral service. One day Stelling mentioned that he had a studio in the East Village he wanted to convert into an art gallery. "I was picking up all this inside knowledge about graffiti from the movie," said Astor. She was convinced graffiti could be sold to serious art collectors, so she helped Stelling organize the Fun Gallery. Although it was never intended strictly as a graffiti gallery, several writers were given shows during the first year, including Brathwaite, Futura, Dondi, and Quinones. Haring and Scharf, two painters who were being influenced by graffiti, were also given shows. At first the graffiti-based paintings didn't sell well, but Astor knew she was onto something when European art dealer Bruno Bischofberger rolled in from Zurich for Brathwaite's opening.

"I didn't even know who he was," said Astor. "He had a babe on each arm and he pulled out these index cards that were crammed with info. He asked who the most important graffiti artists were. Later I found out he's the second biggest collector in the world after Count Panza. I immediately decided I wanted to be like Bruno."

Unfortunately, many writers found it difficult, if not impossible, to make the transition from guerrilla outlaw to studio painter. Graffiti murals depended largely on size, color, and constant movement, and the work lost much of its impact when put on small, static canvases. To make matter worse, a number of entrepreneurs began selling graffiti paintings as if they were charming folk art trinkets. The Fun Gallery became a notable exception to this trend, since Astor encouraged the writers to consider themselves serious artists. She provided a refreshing alternative to the sometimes pompous Soho art scene, where openings tended to be stody, boring and predictable. Openings at the Fun, on the other hand, were filled with wild energy and an eclectic mix of downtown celebrities, b-boys, and art collectors.

It wasn't long before a few writers, notably Quinones and Futura, began working with imagery that translated well onto canvas. But the big break came in November 1982, when a cover story by Rene Ricard appeared in *Artforum*. For the past three years, Ricard had been cultivating a reputation for being at the cutting edge of the art scene, having successfully predicted the rise of such painters as Julian Schnabel and Jean-Michel Basquiat. Many collectors were watching Ricard closely to see if he would tell them what the "next thing" would be. They weren't disappointed. Ricard, who had appeared with Astor in *Underground USA*, wrote:

Patti Astor is a beautiful example of what John Ashbery would call 'An Exhilarating Mess' in operation. She isn't a businesswoman: she's currently starring in Charlie Ahearn's movie 'Wild Style,' and the opening of the gallery coincided with (or caused) a definite shift in the social pattern of the last two years. The underground movie scene played itself out. The rock scene, sperm of the great club period in the second half of the '70s, has run to water, losing the music war and now, except for a few skin-head arsenals, barely exists. Painting became big news....When Futura 2000 or Dondi White walk into a club it sparks the same sparks usually reserved for rock or movie stars. Economics have influenced this power shift; new bands don't make the kind of money that very young painters do. The winning musicians are DJs, and they play wheels of steel, not guitars...

In Lee Quinones' June 1982 exhibit at the old Fun (it moved during the summer) was a painting as radical and as difficult as it was pretty and decorative. It depicts a bird on a cliff in front of a nuclear sunset. It is spray-painted on tin in what could be termed

'Van Style.' The bird, the dove of peace, is like a cartoon character that we are already familiar with. It has the same recognition impact as a Donald Duck, but a Donald Duck who has failed and who, without melodrama, confronts the viewer with embarrassed helplessness. Everything about this picture defies currently approved tradition. It is extremely sentimental. It looks like a poster. It has no brushstrokes. Like all of Quinones' work this painting is the product of a personal and introspective sensibility that has earned him the reputation of a seer and prophet.

In the small, insular New York art scene, *Artforum* wields a tremendous amount of clout, and soon after Ricard's article appeared, the Fun Gallery no longer had trouble attracting collectors. In fact, Astor's biggest problem was holding on to her artists. Quinones joined the Barbara Gladstone Gallery on 57th Street, while Haring and Scharf, both heavily courted by several dealers, joined the Shafrazi Gallery in Soho. Haring, Basquiat, and Quinones were invited to exhibit at Documenta 7, a prestigious international art show held in Kassel, West Germany, while other graffiti writers began appearing in various galleries on 57th Street, once a bastion for conservative, blue-chip art. It may have been started by a hodge-podge of impoverished art school dropouts and unschooled graffiti writers, but by 1982 they had turned it into the hottest art movement in America.

Chapter 6: Breaking Out

In 1976, Tito and Macho were members of the RCA Rockmasters, a crew of Puerto Rican teenagers based near the Tremont section of the Bronx around 180th Street and Southern Boulevard. Like many crews during the period, RCA started as a group of fun-loving disco dancers. Unfortunately, as the group got larger, they began acting more and more like a streetgang. Tito and Macho were not comfortable being in a gang, so they convinced several friends to quit RCA and form their own crew. "One night we made a big pile of our RCA sweatshirts and burned them. Then we started thinking about a new name. I said, 'How about "Rockwell"?' Everybody liked that, so we became the Rockwell Association."

The group included Willie, Carlos, Victor, Hector, Pops, Rubberband, George, and Shorty. They were a Puerto Rican crew during a time when communication between blacks and Puerto Ricans was somewhat limited. Both groups were into music and dance, both threw block parties, but the similarities stopped there. Puerto Ricans played disco music, while blacks played hard-core funk. Puerto Ricans dressed in flower-print shirts and pointy-toed shoes and danced the Hustle, while blacks wore bell-bottoms and sneakers while break dancing. However, around 1977, a Puerto Rican deejay named Charlie Chase helped bring about a merger of the two styles.

"From 1974 to 1977 I was in a band at Alfred E. Smith High School," said Chase. "But then I got interested in deejaying. There was a crew around my house called the Monterey Crew. they were the first I saw getting into the b-boy style. They didn't do any fancy cutting with their music, but they played 'Just Begun' and records like that. My deejay friends would only play disco music, which was all right, but it didn't really turn on the crowds like 'Just Begun.' So, I started doing a little deejaying. My friends would say, 'Okay Charlie, here's your turn to play your black music,' and I would get fifteen minutes to do my thing. When I was on the set, everybody would dance and my friends couldn't understand why."

Willie Will was 16 at the time and had just learned to break dance. "Pops taught me," he said, referring to a friend a year younger than himself. "He learned from the Zulus. They had one dancer named Chopper who was real good. Breaking was like a hobby. We'd go into a hallway and practice until three or four in the morning. Get drunk. Fight. There was nothing else to do. I don't know where the spinning came from, but it was out in 1976. The Zulus had footwork, headspins, backspins. We used to break on the concrete in Belmont Park. If you did a backspin, you'd only spin around once or twice. Everybody was in crews and the crews would break against each other. First the whole crew would dance and then the best one from each crew would go down."

After developing the dance for over five years, many blacks grew tired of breaking and had stopped by 1978. Some got into the Hustle or the Freak. Others did the Electric Boogie, a robotic mime-like dance popular in California and down South. However, the Puerto Ricans were just getting into breaking and had no intention of giving it up. Saint Martin's, a Catholic church located on 182nd Street and Crotona Avenue, began sponsoring breaking battles in their gymnasium with the local priests acting as judges. Well-known crews participating in the battles included The Disco Kids (TDK), the Apache Crew, Star Child La Rock, and TBB. However, the Rockwells were widely considered the best.

"We beat everybody," said Macho calmly. "There was nobody else to challenge. The next year they picked the best guys from each crew to gang up on us. TBB had Bobby Lee, Spy, Track and Mongo. Spy and Willie were always going throat to throat."

"Believe it or not, I used to hang out with Spy," said Willie. "We used to practice together. One day I did a swipe and landed on my head. I was trying to work out a new routine. 'Do a headspin! Do a headspin!' said Spy. He helped me find a new move."

The final showdown of the Rockwells versus TBB and the reat of the Bronx was held at Saint Martin's during the summer of 1979. "The place was packed," said Macho. "They had chairs arranged in a circle. We had ten dancers. They had about twenty-five. Everything came down to Willie and George against Spy and Mongo. Then the priests said, Okay, one more move: Spy against Willie. Willie flipped the coin and Spy went first. We did a sweep, messed up and fell down. The crowd booed. Then it was Willie's turn."

"I did my new routine," said Willie. "I started with a split, into a tumble, into a swipe, into a headspin. I got him with the same move he told me to do! Hahahaha. I bet he regretted that one!"

"We won the trophy," said Macho, "but the other crew didn't want to admit we won. They said it was fixed. They said we bought the fathers! They wanted to fight. See, breaking is not only breaking. There's a lot of fighting too. You go to a party and burn this guy and he says, 'You want to battle, man? Let's battle with the hands. You're a punk,' and this and that. Then you go outside and find fifty dudes waiting for you. TDK was like that. They always looked at us wrong and would never speak to us."

After the Saint Martin's battle, many of the Rockwells felt they were too old to continue rolling around on concrete, getting skin cuts and tearing their clothes. Tito and Macho bought a sound system and became deejays. "A lot of young kids still wanted to get down with Rockwell," said Macho. "Richie Colon used to hang out. He wanted to get down, but we wouldn't let him 'cause he was too young. His cousin Lennie was down. Then I heard Richie moved to Manhattan and we didn't see him for a while. He said he wanted to form a part of Rockwell in Manhattan."

Colon, a soft-spoken, polite 14-year-old, had spent two years practicing the dance and was just getting good enough to join Rockwell when everyone stopped breaking. He must have felt cheated. Then he moved to Manhattan and discovered that many of the kids around his new neighborhood didn't even know what breaking was. He tried to teach a few, but it wasn't like the old days. Breaking didn't make much sense if you didn't have a rival to battle against. Despite being isolated from his former friends in the Bronx, Colon remained a devoted b-boy. He had never met Kool Herc, Bambaataa or Flash, but he always spoke reverently of them and of all the original breaking crews. He dreamed of forming his own crew someday, one that would be just as famous as the Zulu Kings, the Rockwells, or TBB. He changed his name to Crazy Legs, kept practicing, and spent every weekend traveling around Manhattan looking for breakers. He finally found some on a playground at the corner of 98th Street and Amsterdam Avenue. "I met Ty Fly first," said Crazy Legs. "He introduced me to Ken Rock, Frosty Freeze, Doze, Mania and Take 1. I went against all of them. I'm not gonna even say what happened 'cause they later became my crew."

Meanwhile, Henry Chalfant was exploring the possibilities of publishing a book on graffiti with Martha Cooper, a former *New York Post* photographer. "After I met Fred [Brathwaite] I became aware of rap music," said Chalfant. "But my first indication of breaking came from Martha. We'd been comparing notes on graffiti for some time and one day she showed me a photo she'd taken in 1978 of a break dancer. She wanted to do a story on breaking but was having trouble finding kids still doing it. At the same time, I was approached about putting on a graffiti performance show at Common Ground. I agreed to do the show and asked Take 1, one of the graffiti writers, about breaking. He said, 'Sure, I break and I know the best crew.' The next day he walked in with Crazy Legs and Frosty Freeze from the Rock Steady Crew." Chalfant was stunned when he saw them dance. "It was amazing that this had been going on for years and nobody knew about it. In fact, it was about to die out when I found it."

The media found out about breaking on April 22, 1981, when the *Village Voice* published a cover story on the dance, written by Sally Banes with photos by Cooper. Although it was still nearly impossible to publish articles on graffiti or rap music, both of which seemed to be universally hated by magazine editors, breaking had immediate appeal for the national press, possibly because a quote in the Voice credited the dance with replacing fighting as an outlet for urban aggression. "In the summer of '78," said Tee, "when you got mad at someone, instead of saying, 'Hey man, you want to fight?' you'd say 'Hey man, you want to rock?'" The statement was not entirely accurate (break dancers were notorious for getting into fights, especially with each other), but it was just the sort of quote that makes good newspaper copy. When the article appeared there were only a handful of breakers left in the city, but within months television camera crews, reporters and independent filmmakers were scouring the city in search of more. The attention lavished on the dancers allowed graffiti writers and rappers to get media exposure as well. Graffiti and rapping were no longer thought of as bizarre, isolated phenomena but as integral parts of a complex subculture.

Until 1981, it was difficult for a white, downtown audience to experience live rap music or see a break-dance contest, because these activities took place well inside the ghetto, where few whites were willing to travel. However, as the popularity of break dancing spread, it became apparent that whites would flock to any club associated with hip hop, as long as the club was located below 96th Street in Manhattan. On Second Avenue around the corner from the original Fun Gallery was a small basement nightclub called Negril, which had been unsuccessfully trying to cultivate an audience for Jamaican music. Ruza Blue, a concert promoter from England, and Michael Holman, an independent film and video maker from California, began throwing hip hop parties at the club on Thursday nights. Herc, Bambaataa, the Treacherous Three, the Cold Crush, the Rock Steady Crew, and other hip hop celebrities began appearing at the club, which catered primarily to a white audience—although there were always plenty of Bronx b-boys on hand to give the place an authentic flavor. Negril's greatest moment probably came the night Rock Steady Crew battled Floormasters, a crew from the Bronx later known as the New York City Breakers. For the first time the audience got a taste of the competitive nature of breaking. Rock star David Byrne and painter Francesco Clemente began frequenting Negril, which, because of its small, intimate dance floor, often seemed more like a private party than a night club. Much of the intimacy was lost when the operation was moved to the Roxy, a cavernous roller rink on West 18th Street. However, by 1982 the downtown hip hop scene had gotten far too big for a tiny club like Negril.

Much of the credit for the growing acceptance of hip hop was undoubtedly due to Robert Christgau of the *Voice* and Robert Palmer of the *New York Times*, two of the most influential rock critics in New York at the time. Both were early supporters of rap music. For several years Christgau and Palmer were among the only mainstream rock critics regularly reviewing 12-inch rap singles put out by small, independent labels. On March 25, 1981, Christgau's "Consumer Guide" column in the *Voice*, once a bastion for progressive rock albums, contained reviews of no fewer than six rap records. These critics realized that hip hop was the first progressive movement to appear in black music in several years, and that it had the potential to cross over to a wider audience.

In 1981, Bambaataa had just established a relationship with a fledgling label called Tommy Boy Records when he began deejaying at clubs like Negril and the Mudd Club. He immediately went to work on a record designed to appeal to the new wave crowd as well as hip hoppers. Under the guidance of producer Arthur Baker, he raided musical fragments from sources appreciated by both groups: the pioneering German synthesizer band Kraftwerk, the film The Good, the Bad, and the Ugly, Captain Sky, and Babe Ruth. A Roland TR 808 drum computer replaced a studio drummer, and the musical track was provided by a single keyboard player, John Robie. The result, titled "Planet Rock," unalterably changed the sound of dance music for the next two years.

"Planet Rock" was released in May 1982 and, according to Billboard, was "an instant club and retail hit of formidable size, shipping near-gold upon release." Part of the success of the record was due to a new style of rap, which appeared on the record for the first time. Invented by G.L.O.B.E., a member of Soul Sonic Force, the rap was the result of years of experimentation. "The problem with a lot of rappers is they were stuck in the Bo Diddley syndrome," said G.L.O.B.E. "They just wanted to brag about themselves. I was working on something different and when I showed it to Bam, he really liked it." The lyrics were a dreamy, utopian throwback to the sixties, with lines like: "You're in a place where the nights are hot/where nature's children dance and say the chants/of this mother earth which is our rock/The time has come it was foretold, to show you really got soul."

G.L.O.B.E. also created a new style of rapping to augment the lyrics. "I call it MC Popin'," he said. "It's a step above rapping and a little less than singing. It's an acrobatic way of saying words. The tongue moves faster and it has more melody to it. Today a lot of people imitate it but MC Poppin' in mine. I invented it in 1978."

Richard Grabel, New York correspondent for the British newspaper *New Musical Express*, began writing extensively about rap music, which found a devoted following in England, where rock groups imitated the "Planet Rock sound" using Roland drum computers and synthesizer effects. The Clash hired Futura 2000 to paint backdrops during their performances, shows that often ended with Futura climbing down from his ladder, throwing aside his can of spray paint, and rapping his own song, "The Escapades of Futura 2000."

In 1981, Chris Frantz and Tina Weymouth, both members of the rock band Talking Heads, formed the Tom Tom Club, a group that specialized in a pop-oriented, electro-funk sound. They recorded an intellectual rap single titled "Wordy Rappinghood," followed by the more successful "Genius of Love," which became an extremely influential record in the world of hip hop. Ed Fletcher, resident percussionist for Sugarhill Records, would soon design a musical track inspired in large part by "Genius of Love" and offer it to Grandmaster Flash and the Furious Five.

"At first, nobody wanted to do the song 'cause it was too low down," said Melle Mel. "The basic structure of rap is to get people to participate in a party, and all the rappers, including us, were scared to try something more serious. Why take your problems into a disco? I think Sylvia Robinson was the only one who really believed in the song. Ed Fletcher had the concept for two years and never did anything with it, but Miss Robinson knew it would be a big record and convinced us to do it."

Actually, the merger of rap with a serious message had first successfully taken place in 1980 with the release of "How We Gonna Make the Black Nation Rise?" by Brother D and the Collective Effort. Brother D (whose real name was Daryl Aamaa Nubyahn) was a member of the New York Family of National Black Science, a revolutionary organization "dedicated to the uplifting of black people and to the acquiring of knowledge and skills."

"I noticed kids around my block in the Bronx doing rap, but there was no message," said Nybyahn. "I was teaching math in a vocational training program and I started running some raps for the kids in my class. I made deals with them like, you do a certain amount of work and I'll rap for you at the end of the period. And they loved that. There was a strong desire in rap records for people to soup themselves up. Big fantasies—folks in their teens talking about my big car, I'm a movie star, I've got all the women in the world. People are very materially centered. Something flashes on TV and they have to go out and get it. With the idea of hooking rap up with political information and the practice I got rapping for my students, I began to write."

Set to a musical track taken from Cheryl Lynn's disco hit "Got to Be Real," Nybyahn repeated an angry refrain: "We're rising up, we won't take no more! We're rising up we won't take no more!" Although it was an explosively effective record, it was far too political to ever attain wide popularity in hip hop circles. By 1982, when Grandmaster Flash and the Furious Five went into the studio to record their own version of a "serious" rap record, they hadn't even heard of Brother D and Collective Effort.

Fletcher became the principal architect of "The Message," a song that would soon become rap's greatest single. Although his lyrics carried an emotional intensity equal to "How We Gonna Make the Black Nation Rise?" Fletcher left out the political ideology. The persona portrayed in the song was that of a typical South Bronx resident pressured to the point of desperation by his environment. "Don't push me, I'm close to the edge," warns the voice. "I'm trying not to lose my head. It's like a jungle sometimes, it makes me wonder, how I keep from going under." The cause for this tension was graphically illustrated: "Broken glass everywhere, people pissing on the stairs, you know they just don't care. I can't take the smell, I can't take the noise. Got no money to move out, I guess I got no choice. Rats in the front room, roaches in the back. Junkies in the alley with the baseball bat. I tried to get away but I couldn't get far, because the man from Prudential repossessed my car."

Fletcher and Mel took turns reciting the lyrics on the record, carefully juxtaposing their voices for a unique effect. Fletcher provided a more low-key, disco-style rap, which served to heighten the angry aggressiveness of Mel's delivery. In fact, by varying his tones, inserting slight, dramatic pauses, and occasionally speeding up his tempo to create a sense of urgency, Mel gave a performance as meticulously planned and executed as any aria, completing the song with a rap he wrote in 1980 describing the birth, decline and eventual death in prison of a South Bronx hoodlum, a story told in sharp, cinematic imagery. A rapping tour de force, "The Message" stands as one of the most powerful poetic performances ever captured on vinyl.

"The Message" received the maximum rating of five stars from Rolling Stone, where Kurt Loder called it "the most detailed and devastating report from underclass America since Bob Dylan decried the lonesome death of Hattie Carroll—or, perhaps more to the point, since Marvin Gaye took a long look around and wondered what was going on." Several months later it topped nearly every critic's list as best single of the year. "Planet Rock" may have provided the musical inspiration for the further development of hip hop, but it was "The Message" that created the impetus for greater lyrical complexity. Appropriately, the song that represented one of hip hop's finest moments described the South Bronx, the territory where hip hop began.

"No one I know in New York learned about hip hop from movies or books," says Phase 2 today. "We experienced it all around us and through us. From the Lindy Hop and Jitterbug, to the Boogaloo, Afro Twist, Latin Hustle and freestyle, you always had those who were taking it all to a different level. Older brothers and sisters rocked to mother Popcorn and Karate Boogaloo at a sweet 16 house party. Just because you write or were in a movie or a book doesn't make you hip hop, just like being able to spin on your head doesn't necessarily make you a b boy. For the true hardcore, it's deeper and more spiritual. Words like "legend," "old school" and "pioneer" are not appropriated correctly these days."

The Great Phase 2

I'd completely forgotten about my first interview with graffiti legend Phase 2, always a mysterious and hard-to-find character—and even more today than when Sisco Kid helped me track him down in the early 1980s.

I remember Phase came all the way down to the offices of the East Village Eye with me while the art director was laying out the story so we could take a portrait of him for the article. While we were there, I convinced Phase to make an illustrated history of graffiti off the top of his head and I sat there watching him on deadline telling him to hurry up. Meanwhile, Phase is trying to do his best to honor some of the greatest tags in history. It's amazing how effortlessly he pulled that assignment off.

I'm pretty sure the art director at the time was Dave Allen, an English dude who'd just arrived in NYC via Los Angeles. It was Dave who told German photographer Andre Grossmann that he should start hanging around with me, as I was onto sometime really big, which I was. Andre took a portrait of Phase for the article and it was the beginning of our collaboration, which would intensify after I moved over to *High Times*.

Craig Castleman's book on graffiti had just been published and praised in the *New Yorker* by one of my favorite writers, Calvin Tomkins, but I found the book riddled with disinfo. Instead of interviewing the top dudes, which is what I was trying to do, the book relied on comments by toys and lesser talents, some of whom (according to Phase) had a distorted view of graffiti history.

Soon, I would be talking with Harry Belafonte about producing my film script "Looking for the Perfect Beat," which mixed up real stories about Futura 2000 and Phase 2 (two of my favorite writers, although from different generations). I also got a book deal with St. Martins' Press, although they never knew what to do with the first history of hip hop and actually cataloged it as a "dance book" because it came out as break-dancing arrived. Castleman called me up in a frenzy when he read my book and accused me of ripping him off, even though his book never really delved into anything but graffiti and was nothing like mine at all. Even so, I'd done a better job with graffiti history than he did, though, and I guess he knew it. And it was up to me to lay out the history of the gangs, the environment that helped spawn the culture, and how gang style evolved into hip hop after people got tired of violence and wanted to just have fun again. There were a lot of people like Castleman hovering around graffiti at the time, but not noticing rap music, break dancing and a whole new style of talking and walking were exploding in the Bronx.

The funniest part was how the Belafonte production team got swarmed by black dudes from Brooklyn who insisted hip hop started in Brooklyn and that Phase 2 and the other dudes I was promoting were really complete nobodies. In fact, when Phase delivered his one line in the final movie, at the big free screening arranged for all Harry's buddies, Phase was actually booed by many in the crowd? Holy cow, what were they thinking? After the screening Alisha, Harry's assistant pointed out those boos as if it was some sort of condemnation of my perspective, or maybe just her rationalization for jettisoning me. After all, they didn't use my script and the result was a disaster. I only wish someday, someone would actually produce the original script I wrote, which anyone can read on smashwords. Read my story, then go watch the movie and tell me something terrible didn't go awry with *Beat Street.*

"I first met Phase in 1973, shortly after I founded United Graffiti Artists. The first half of graffiti was primarily execution: quantity, bravado, risks, etc., but the second half was based on style. I'd heard about a writer named Phase 2, who had so many styles that he was giving them out to other writers. I knew he was the major influence in the Bronx, so I invited him to UGA. When he came in

the door, it was obvious I was dealing with an amazing creative source. His energy was all over the place. His body was alive; the place was bopping. What do I think of Phase today? I think he's a genius. I think he's the godfather of style." Hugo Martinez, Oct. 1982

Exactly ten years ago, the first organized attempt to market subway graffiti as art began when Hugo Martinez invited 12 writers to spray-paint a 10 x 40 foot paper-covered wall at City College. Martinez's efforts to legitimize graffiti eventually fizzled and most people expected the "fad" to fizzle along with it.

It didn't happen. Graffiti went back underground, periodically surfacing at various galleries and alternative spaces around New York. Recently, graffiti has been invigorated by its connection with hip hop music. It has been hyped in *Art In America*, *Art Forum*, *Arts Magazine* and *Art News*. It has been widely imitated by art students. In fact, graffiti seems destined to take its rightful place in art history.

But where is this place?

Before anyone will determine the answer, both factions of our current graffiti controversy will have to cool down and take a close look at what is covering the walls and subway trains of this city. At this point, blanket acceptance is no more helpful than blanket condemnation. There can be no doubt that most graffiti being done today is boring and poorly executed. But the same could be said for most art. The only notable difference is that bad artists have difficulty foisting their sensibility on an unreceptive audience, while bad graffiti writers find it relatively easy. The true promise and potential of graffiti has always resided in the work of a small core of master writers. Remove the contribution of these few writers and one is left with an exciting, daredevil sport—but no art to speak of. And no other single writer has contributed more to the history of graffiti as art than Phase 2, who continues to live an existence of quiet anonymity, despite his legendary status within the subculture.

They say it started in 1969. Contrary to popular belief, the first graffiti writers claim they did not start marking up the city in an attempt to make themselves famous. The wrote because it was fun. At first, no one paid much attention to them. It was just a secret little hobby shared by a small band of non-conformists. The introduction of the magic marker in the late sixties had provided the necessary technology, the will had been around since time immemorial.

In the summer of 1971, the New York Times inadvertently created a mini-boom in graffiti when it sent a reporter to find out the mysterious identity of "Taki 183." The reporter tracked down a likeable 17-year-old who said: "You don't do it for the girls. They don't seem to care. You do it for yourself." The article appeared on July 21 and Taki was enshrined forever in the graffiti hall of fame. Who knows how many kids went out the next day and bought magic markers as a result of that story?

Solo graffiti (as distinct from gang graffiti) probably started on the Upper West Side, but it wasn't until the trend moved into the South Bronx that its full potential was realized. By 1971, the graffiti writer was well on his way to becoming the new urban hipster: part outlaw, part artist, part daredevil, its was a synthesis that proved irresistible.

Sly II was the first writer on 163rd Street in the Bronx. He was quickly followed by Lee 163, who developed a uniquely stylized signature, stacking and fusing the letters in his name like a corporate logo. Lee began writing in March 1971. In October, his friend Phase 2 appeared. "Phase had a positive reaction to my graffiti," says Lee. "But he wasn't going to start writing just because I was. He's always had his own mind. He waited until he was ready."

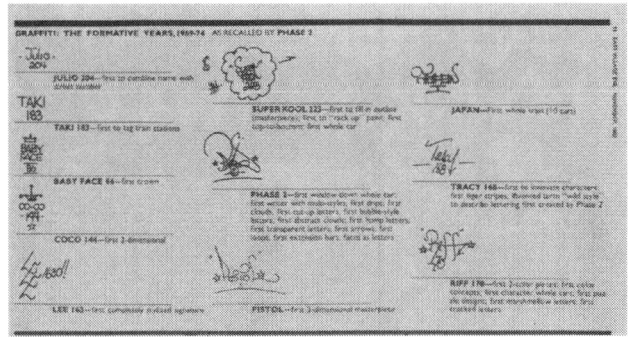

Taggers hall of fame by Phase 2.

"The previous year we'd given this party," explains Phase. "We were getting ready to give another party and I said, we'll call this one phase two. It was like I discovered something, like it was destiny. I don't know why, but I was stuck on the name. It had meaning for me."

Phase worked his way into the subculture slowly. It wasn't until he visited the West Side and saw Cay 161's work that he became obsessed with "bombing." "Cay was a fucking madman," he says. "When I saw what he was doing, I said, "This is the way it's supposed to be done. I'm going back up to the Bronx and tear shit up. I became a madman 'cause I was kinda sick too. People write for different reasons, but there's basically two types. Either you're in or you're not. Either you're dedicated or you're not. Graffiti has meaning for me, it holds strength. It's not some bullshit. I was out there because I wanted to bomb, man! Another ten years from now, the guys that are really dedicated will still be saying, yeah, I remember when we used to ride the trains."

At the time, Phase was tall, skinny and almost always wore a hat jauntily perched on his head. A French cap made by Flechet was his favorite. He projected an almost explosive sense of urgency; his occasional stuttering heightening the impression his physical being was struggling to keep pace with a galloping imagination. While talking, he frequently twisted and clenched his fingers, as if creating a pattern for some bizarre new lettering style. He was outgoing and seemed to know everyone in the Bronx. "You couldn't walk down the street with him without his saying hello to a dozen people," says one friend. Few people, however, knew Phase was a writer.

"I tried to keep a low profile," he says. "For quite a while nobody knew I was Phase 2. I told my friends not to tell anyone. That was the fun of it. You could sit around and people would say, Damn, you know who I want to meet? Phase 2. And I'd be sitting right next to them."

In 1973, Super Kool 223 revolutionized graffiti by spraying large outlines of his signatures on the outside of trains, outlines that were painstakingly filled in with paint. "Everybody was damn negative about it at first," says Phase. "Even I thought the shit was crazy. It took a whole can of paint! With one can you could write your name so many damn times. But then everybody picked up on it. I remember seeing some block letters by Sentry 120. That's when I came out with my softie letters. People started calling it the bubble style."

The giant signatures became known as "masterpieces" and it suddenly became necessary to steal a lot of paint in order to execute them.

"Super Kool and his girl friend were the first to rack up huge quantities," says Phase. "He was always dressed very dapper. He didn't look the type. But stealing went along with the graffiti shit. I didn't get into it, but a lot of guys did. Not just paint, but leather coats, stereos. One time I led about 20 guys into a store. We went straight to the paint. Something came over me. I slapped all the cans off the shelf. It was crazy. There was so much confusion. Guys were screaming. The salesman tried to keep us in the store. Guys had to throw blows to get out. The mounted police came. We ran around the corner and had four cans of paint between 20 guys. That wasn't the way to do it."

In October of 1972, Hugo Martinez, a sociology student at City College, founded United Graffiti Artists (UGA), a quasi-democratic organization designed to take the master writers off the street and provide them with a more professional environment. "At first the group was all Puerto Rican except for one Greek," says Martinez. "Three or four members did not want to accept blacks. I knew the black writers from the Bronx represented the birth of the masterpiece, so I tried to manipulate votes and put pressure on certain individuals to bring them into the group."

Getting Up: Subway Graffiti in New York (a book by Craig Castelman published last month) characterizes Martinez as a racist who was very reluctant to allow blacks into UGA. Martinez, who was not interviewed for the book, hotly denies the allegation.

"The first graffiti writers were members of gangs," he says. "I was dealing with a few gang members whose biggest enemy was the Bronx. I couldn't be overt about what I was doing."

One thing is certain: there was a tremendous amount of racial tension at UGA, which was unusual since most writers at the time respected each other regardless of color. "I think he favored the

Puerto Ricans," says Lee 163rd. "Sometimes he would hold meetings with them and we wouldn't find out about it until later."

The tension eventually flared into a full-scale rumble at UGA headquarters on Jumel Place at 168th Street. UGA member Henry 161 showed up one day accompanied by five or six members of the Young Galaxies, a local street gang. They immediately began trashing the studio. "I got hit in the head with a stick," says Phase. "Hugo did too. It was fucking crazy. Henry got kicked out of the group. I later found out certain writers felt threatened by us."

There were other problems, like the controversy between Snake I and Snake 131. Snake 131 was considered to be the original Snake and to prove it, he started writing Snake I-131.

It was too much for Snake I to bear. He went to Snake 1`31's house armed with a revolver. "It wasn't like they didn't like each other," says Phase. "They were both members of the group. Snake I just said: Drop the fucking one and left." Fortunately, Snake 131 dropped it.

Why did the writers take their efforts so seriously? "We were devoted 'cause it belonged to us," says Phase. "It was ours. Nobody could take it away from us."

In the three years of UGA's existence, several exhibitions were held. Phase 2 and AMRL (also known as Bama) established themselves as the most talented painters. Both sold canvases in the $2,000 price range. Phase was the major stylistic innovator; AMRL a superb colorist.

According to one of their own press releases, UGA members had stopped writing on trains. This was actually a publicity gimmick intended to smooth over relations with the outside world. Phase had slowed down on hitting the trains, but his concepts always found their way to the yards, primarily through Riff 170. "They fed off each other," says Martinez. "They were like Lennon and McCartney. They were a synthesis of style and execution. Riff had a photographic memory. They say he had a shutter in his eye. Phase got his source from inside. He might be influenced by other things, but you never really know where he gets his ideas. How he conceptualizes things is beyond me."

Phase was continually altering his lettering style. He would fuse letters, extend them, twist them, elongate them. The letters got increasingly ornate and experimental. The style was extremely popular with other writers in the Bronx and soon became a dominant force in graffiti. A writer named Tracy 168 picked up on it and began calling it Wild Style."

Meanwhile, Phase and AMRL accepted scholarships from Pratt, where they studied illustration and commercial art. Phase lasted 3 years before dropping out. "I got a sense of how to execute at Pratt," he says. "The work there was very sophisticated. It didn't really influence the direction of my work, but I was aware of the quality of what they were doing. I left because there were too many problems and too much other shit was going on."

The hip hop scene was growing and Phase had become an integral part of it. His dancing style had always been wild and innovative—just like his art—and Phase was a pioneer of break dancing. He began creating flyers for an old fried named Kool Herc, who also wrote graffiti in the early seventies before becoming the first hip hop deejay. "Yeah, graffiti started it all," admits Herc.

"I don't mean to brag," says Phase, "but I knew how to innovate those flyers. I knew how to advertise. Me, Sisco Kid, Buddy Esquire, Riley, Danny T., we helped push those rappers. We hyped them with some really vicious flyers. I think the flyers helped build hip hop. Herc set the pace for the scene but the first real rapping I remember was Cowboy. Flash would play Bongo Rock [real title: Apache by the Incredible Bongo Band] and Cowboy would say: To the rock, rock, rock. South side…make money. East side…make money. It sounded so bad. The impact was there. It made sense and added so much to the music."

Never one to imitate another's style Phase soon developed the crooning rap, a vocal style that combined rap lyrics with real singing. "About three years ago I saw him win a talent show at the Ecstasy Garage," says Kool Herc. "I didn't even know he could sing. He's got a good voice. He's just waiting for his big break."

That break may have arrived. A French record company has recently asked Phase to record for them. If it happens, it can't be soon enough for Phase, who often seems desperate to escape the South Bronx.

"It has changed like crazy," he says. "You don't even want to be here anymore. That's how I feel. The shit started with the blackout in '77. That just totaled the whole damn neighborhood. People ransacked the stores and the businesses never came up out of it. It was the start of something bad. A person with some kind of feelings doesn't belong here anymore. It seems like evil prevails. Everybody has a fucked up attitude. I want to get out, move to some corner of the world where they only kill one person a year. I don't belong in this shit. Everything is a fucking gimmick these days. Everybody is a phony. I respect making money only when people see a purpose for what they're doing. So many writers are thinking out of synch, crossing out each other's names. Before, we had respect. You might hate a guy's guts, thought he was a sucker, but still said, damn, he sure can paint. A lot of these guys today don't realize what we went through. We went from one stage to the next at random. The skeleton of graffiti has been out since '76. All the shit was laid down. I think what they're doing today is fucking crazy. Too much marking on the insides. It looks pathetic."

It seems strange that despite his privileged status in graffiti history, Phase 2 has not had a gallery show in over six years. This oversight is primarily due to the fact that he has never pushed his work. He still draws continuously, however, and his latest sketches represent the cutting edge of the new alien machine style. "I relate to unearthly things," he says. "You might think it's crazy, but I think I had a previous life in Egypt. That's where I get a lot of my ideas."

In 2012, I asked Phase if I could interview him again, only on video. He declined, but did release the following statement:

"Having a vision beyond the basics did a lot to build street culture. So much BS has been written that it's taken the realness out of context. I grew up in an atmosphere where we recognized that we were being denied and robbed of knowledge of culture and knowledge of self. Overstanding that I've intensified my instinct to look into things even further. Unfortunately too many people don't realize the true essence of the culture, it's foundations and the heart of those who made it happen and stood by it religiously. We created an art form that came up from our supposedly insignificant existences and now it's everywhere on earth. That's a testament in itself. In the the late 60's amidst an abundance of political and social turmoil, cultural awareness, racial pride and unrest, a youth-inspired movement emerged from New York. Those who spawned it's birth called it writing. Writing and the aerosol art movement as we know it today, its elements, its hows, its whys began in New York City all by it's lonesome. It was never influenced by any other so-called writer movements anywhere else on the planet earth. If we didn't do it here it wouldn't exist as you are witnessing it. If it has a founding father or fathers, or anyone to pay homage to, they, without a doubt, come from New York. So kill all the lies, myth, noise and the nonsense!

I'm not trying to disrespect or toot my own horn but I was always doing my thing. For example, I danced. I could draw. I played b ball. I was under 6 foot tall just before my 15th birthday dunking above regulation rims. The school system deemed me to be smarter than average. I'm not ego tripping and I don't concoct stories. I'm just trying to make a point. I didn't need my name on a subway car to tell me that I was a bit nice. The name of the game was getting up. I started doing it because someone I rolled with on the daily was down with it. So many guys created and developed a signature and name to suit them and be original and independent. That was part of what you wanted to establish. You could easily see some type of a personality or flavor in the signatures of a Superkool 223 or a Jec Star, Cay 161, LEE 163d!, Slim one, Kool Kito, King Of Kools, Dino Nod, Tye 24. Some of these names seemed resounding and the signatures were in their own way no less then dignified and quite amazing. Writing had guidlines rules and regulations. Do's and don'ts. Respect the name. No writing over one another. Start nothing there'll be nothing. Don't mess with me, I won't mess with you. Give everyone their space to rock accordingly. So we had ethics. I seem to have always connected to the things that I could elaborate and innovate off of. Dancing. Drawing. Balling. You could always flip it how you wanted to. Long before I wrote, I realized that I didn't like the way I was taught to do it and once I realized I didn't have to do it that way, it gave me a wider and more imaginative view of rendering it. You have to think what if there was no Super Kool or Riff 170? Would there be the masterpieces on trains, top to bottoms, fat caps, ill designs, certain funky styles or what have you? What you see these days was basically blueprinted in the 70's and run with into the 80's up 'till now. The technical aspects are different, but there's no way that you could have any of this without firstly the signature and the style formations and piecing approaches that were done then. In the late 80's, you had major developments that came out of the West Coast with guys like Slic and Hex that changed the whole approach to technique and that has also become a staple in the culture. Almost like a second blueprint that has also been adapted globally. It all started out with little magic markers. And evidently progressed and developed into something way out of control and much bigger than that. It's a crazy occurance. We're a part of something that is not only a part of New York history...but a part of the world. Instead of trying to deal with the culture, the authorities chose to wipe it out. Just think...they tried to kill it, but it just wouldn't die. No one I know here in New York "learned" about hip hop from movies or books. We experienced it all around us and through us. From the Lindy Hop and Jitterbug, to the Boogaloo, Afro Twist, Latin Hustle and freestyle, you always had those who were taking it all to a different level. Older brothers and sisters rocked to mother Popcorn and Karate Boogaloo at a sweet sixteen house party. They got to watch the sly slick and wicked cats in their alpaca sweaters and gators looking suave boogying with the fly girls and then cooling out to a slow jam. We didn't call what we did breaking in the sense that it was a dance. It was just slang. One of the main terminologies was to "go off" or going off" and to "turn out." "Rocking" was just another terminology meaning "to get down." If your moms was breaking on you she wouldn't be dancing, she'd be hollering above level and we didn't "break dance" either. That's someone else's terminology. We "broke" when it came time to flip the script on the floor beyond the norm. Breaking in it's initial hey day came out of dance basics and freestyle dancing. We'd go to parties and bug out and get noticed. And it was obvious that we had something that others didn't when a girl would comment. "I've never seen anyone dance like y'awll." I had another idea that none of us had ever seen any dancers from anywhere else doing, which was a five to six step motion where we pretended to have knives in our hands (ala West Side Story) and swing in left to right motions like we were fighting. We'd then kick out bend down or squat drop, come back up and body nod or shake the head in an aggressive motion. That was like a trademark dance of ours. I call it Battle Rocking but we never really bothered to name it. Then it was back to freestyling and doing the dance of the month. In our area it died with everything else because there was nothing subtle about it. When I saw kids still breaking years later it was one form they were calling Up Rocking. A lot of dances come out and we never know who started them, we just do them. But in this case we moved around town and were so addicted into rocking that we always knew what we brought to the table because it was that personal and we saw it disperse even amongst the most known dancers and b boys who were getting shout outs doing some of our moves. A lot of us never really considered ourselves as b boys because basically that was a title reserved for Kool Herc's boys. He coined the phrase. I acknowledge everyone who was noticed from all around the scene. Little Johnny, Sa-sa, Clark Kent, El Dorado Mike, The Twins, James Bond, Amazing Bo Bo, Mr. Bubble, Doris and Janis to name a select few. Just because you write or were in a movie or a book doesn't make you hip hop, just like being able to spin on your head doesn't necessarily make you a b boy. For the true hardcore, it's deeper and more spiritual. Words like legend, old school and pioneer are a joke these days.

Bugging Out on the Endless Peak

Monica from Tommy Boy Records wanted me to check out the Fun House. "Arthur Baker and John Robie are hanging out there all the time," she said. After writing the first story on hip hop in the *Village Voice*, Monica felt I should turn my attention to the way break dancing was spreading out of the South Bronx and into the other boroughs.

The first night I arrived at the club, Randy, the lighting guy, offered to introduce me to Madonna right off the bat. At the time, she was the girl friend of the house deejay, Jellybean, and already had a reputation as a voluptuous siren. I probably said, "naw, that's okay."

See, I was just finishing my book on the origins of hip hop, and I'd already heard the electro-bubblegum sound Madonna was working on. In the early stages of any new cultural wave, its often very hard to distinguish the truly talented, from the talentless opportunists (who always rush in). Aside from the bubblegum melody, Madonna's voice didn't sound all that impressive to me. But, then, I'd never met Madonna in person—or seen her perform.

That night Madonna came up behind me and started talking to me like we were old friends. I was wearing a Levi vest that East Village artist Ellen Berkenblit had customized with one of her iconic punk ponys in white marker on leather. Ellen was a very obscure artist, but one Rene Ricard was currently gushing over. Rene was already famous for "launching" Julian Schnabel and Jean-Michel Basquiat.

"Ellen, right?" she said.

"Uh, yeah." I mumbled, keeping my full attention elsewhere.

After researching the NYC streetgangs, I made my own gang jacket with the help of artist Ellen Birkenblit.

Madonna wasn't one to stick around where she wasn't wanted. (That night she would tell someone I was probably gay.)

Actually, I'd already decided to base my Fun House article around a girl named Alyse, and the Juice Crew. I had this feeling Jellybean wanted a story mostly about him, and Madonna. Maybe I was channeling the responsibilities of power regarding my status as a *Village Voice* cover-story writer. I'm sure I came off as arrogant at best.

Later that week, however, I got to see Madonna perform on stage at the Fun House with her backup dancers. She was amazing and captured my full respect immediately. She obviously had a gift for choreography and oozed with youthful sex appeal. I knew right then she was going to be a star. I suddenly wished I could turn that unfortunate first encounter around, and wondered if that opportunity would ever present itself.

Unfortunately, any plans along those lines were dashed forever the day my Fun House article appeared on the cover of the *Voice*, because the police raided the club early that evening. It just happened to be Jellybean's birthday, and Madonna had a huge party and special command performance planned, so I'd become very unpopular in some circles. A couple of rumors came down the grapevine: "Madonna hates you" and "The Fun House is going to have you knee-capped." Apparently, the club didn't like the references to illegal substances included in my story. Some felt those comments were the reason the police felt compelled to make the raid in the first place.

"Steve Hager's story on the Fun House is still remembered as a classic," Baird Jones would write later in his gossip column. "Although when the expose got that illegal club busted, Steve had to lie very, very low for a few months."

Madonna

I did run into Madonna a few weeks later in the basement dressing room at Danceteria. She looked through me like I didn't exist, while effusively welcoming my sidekick, German photographer

Andre Grossmann. She even let Andre follow her home and take pictures of her in her own environment, until she had to throw him out because he wouldn't *stop* taking pictures. At the time, Andre probably had no clue he was going to make a lot of money off those photographs many years later.

Saturday, 5 p.m.

A pretty, 19-year-old girl named Alyse is standing behind the counter at the Vicenza Pizza Parlor on the corner of Van Wyck Boulevard and Jamaica Avenue in Queens, slapping flour on a wad of pizza dough, anxiously watching the clock, anxious to go home. She has a round face, a squat, muscular body, and wears a gold-plated name tag around her neck. This would be the last Saturday shift for Alyse—it was getting in the way of her dancing.

Enter Mister Glide, a young Puerto Rican and the president of a local break-dance crew known as the Dynamic Rockers. The crew is well-known—they've been in the *Daily News* and the *New York Times* and are negotiating a European tour. Mister Glide wears a sweatshirt, baggies, and flap boots. Studded leather belts are wrapped around his waist, his ankles, his wrists; he looks like a walking S&M shop. Alyse puts a cheese calzone in the oven.

Did you shake it?" he asks.

Alyse giggles. She once told him that her calzones taste the best because she shakes her ass to the music on the radio while she kneads the dough. The more she shakes, the better they taste. Apparently, he likes the idea—every time he comes in he asks the same question.

"Yeah, I shook it," says Alyse.

"You goin' to the Fun House tonight?" he asks. It's a rhetorical question. Alyse always goes to the Fun House on Saturday night. "I think maybe I'll go too," he says.

"The best thing for youse to do," warns Elyse, "is not to go to the Fun House no more." She remembers what happened the last time Dynamic showed up. The Fun House is not their territory.

"Nah, nah," says Mister Glide. "I'll bring my boys. You'll see."

He picks up his calzone, puts $1.50 on the counter and exits. (Mister Glide and his boys, however, will never later appear.) Two hours later, Alyse is home, frantically trying to get ready in time. If she doesn't get to the Fun House by 11, she'll have to pay $12 admission. Before 11, girls get in free. She has less than two hours to shower, dress, and pack her bag. It wouldn't be so bad if there weren't so many minor annoyances to slow her down—like a constantly ringing phone. It's her boyfriend, Nick. He doesn't want her hanging out at the Fun House tonight.

"What!" says Alyse in disbelief. "You can't tell me that! My *father* can't tell me not to go to the Fun House!"

Alyse's mother shakes her head.

"Dancing never help you," she says in a thick Yugoslavian accent. "Want to be somebody? Go to school!"

Alyse laughs. She loves her mother, but what does her mother know about freestyle dancing? Alyse packs her bag first because that's the easiest part. Baby powder, deodorant, two t-shirts, towel, an outfit for the next morning, tennis shoes (for the warm up), leather shoes (for the stage), eyeliner, lipstick, studded belts, earring, toothbrush, toothpaste, cologne, and her "Mama Juice" sweatshirt. That prestigious title was awarded to her after she founded the Juice Crew. Dancing is hard work, especially if you do it for 10 hours at a stretch. Alyse takes a break every few hours, pours baby powder down her back, brushes her teeth, and puts on a fresh shirt. That way, when she walks out of the ladies room, she feels like a new woman.

She grabs a towel and heads for the bathroom. "Ohhh my gawd," she moans. "What am I going to do with my hair?" Her hair is always the biggest problem. Tonight she'll wear a braid.

The Fun House

Saturday 9:45 p.m.

John "Jellybean" Benitez, short, boyishly handsome with long mane of silky black hair, comes in to the Fun House at 526 West 26th Street. Although only 25-years-old, Jellybean has been a professional deejay for over seven years, working at such clubs as Xenon, Hurrah, La Mouche, and New York. In his two years spinning at the Fun House his popularity has skyrocketed, especially among Hispanic and Italian kids from Brooklyn and Queens.

Tonight Jellybean looks a bit distracted. Earlier in the evening his mother was stranded at the airport, and with all the ensuing commotion he forgot to bring an important tape with him, a rough mix of a new record his is producing with his current girlfriend, Madonna, who has yet to be "discovered."

Jellybean never forgave me for leaving him out of my first book on hip hop.

Jellybean stops at the entrance desk and calls a friend in the building, who agrees to bring the tape. Satisfied, Jellybean crosses the dance floor and enters a door marked "private." Located near the door is a 12-foot-high clown's head, complete with a gigantic, three-dimensional nose and yellow lights for eyes. The clown's mouth is open and partially blocked by a glass panel. Before long, Jellybean's face appears in the clown's mouth. It is through this window that he keeps an eye on his audience.

Jellybean looks out on the main dance floor, which has a hard wood surface and is flanked by enormous speaker columns. The back wall and several support columns located throughout the room are sheathed in mirrors. When it's packed, this floor holds over a thousand dancers. To the left of the dance floor is a square four-foot-high platform, which holds several hundred other dancers—it is called the center stage. Past the center stage is an open carpeted area, a bar (no alcohol), a hotdog wagon, an ice cream booth and a smaller circular stage known as the back stage. The back stage holds only 20 to 30 dancers and often features solo performances. A long, narrow balcony overlooks both the center and back stages. Around a corner on the main floor is a game room stocked with 60 video-game machines, including Pac Man and Space Invaders. The room also has an electronic punching bag. For 25 cents a punch, the bag will rate one's punching prowess. Possible scores range from 100 (disaster) to 150 (try again) to 200 (good) to 300 (you're unbeatable). At 300 points, an ear-splitting siren erupts. Altogether, it's about 28,000 feet of space.

Randy Murray, who runs the light show every weekend, comes into the deejay booth and stands next to Jellybean, who is bent over three Technics 1200 turntables, all with records spinning. The crowd is beginning to filter in and Jellybean is cuing his first record of the night. Murray notices a dancer pouring talcum powder on the floor in front of the booth. Murray shakes his head incredulously. "That's his spot," he says. "He's gonna dance on that spot until eight o'clock tomorrow morning."

Sunday 12:45 a.m.

A dozen beefy, musclebound bouncers are standing near the entrance, frisking males for weapons and turning away unwanted customers. Near the bouncers is a red alarm bell that goes off whenever a fight breaks out on the dance floor—something that takes place at least twice a night. Fights can spread faster than a brushfire through the Fun House, so the bouncers need to act quickly. The offending parties are usually tossed into the street within seconds of hitting on each other.

The secret to this system is a network of closed-circuit TV cameras which continually scan the Fun House. Somewhere deep inside the building is a fortified bunker where one of the four owners (Joe, Ronnie, Jerry or Vinnie) sits looking at a bank of video monitors and counting the money delivered into the room straight from the box office via a pneumatic tube. The room has an entrance guarded by a pair of steel doors that open into each other, and make it impossible for more than one person to enter at a time. The Fun House started in 1979 as a gay disco. Then straight kids started coming. Now it's popular with the break dancer/electric boogie scene.

When Arthur Baker and John Robie arrive they are immediately spotted by Angelo, the head bouncer, and ushered though a VIP entrance. Baker and Robie fight their way through a crowd near the center stage, passing a line of girls from Ozone Park who are doing leg kicks and singing along with the music. No one recognizes the two men edging through the crowd, even though Baker and Robie are responsible for five songs played in the last three hours. A year ago, the pair collaborated with Afrika Bambaataa and Soul Sonic Force on the first electronic hip hop record, "Planet Rock." The record quickly became a Fun House classic and spawned a genre of music Baker calls "electro-boogie." Since then, Baker and Robie have tested all their mixes on the Fun House crowd. If the song doesn't go over here, they go back to the studio and rework it. The Fun House has been good to them. So good, in fact, that they are known in dance music circles as "the gurus."

"I really feel the Spanish kids are the trendsetters over the black kids now," says Baker. Tonight many blacks are arriving early and most are turned away with the explanation that the club is "private."

Baker is a huge, hulking man who could pass for a Grateful Dead roadie, but he tends to be quiet and reserved. Robie, on the other hand, is a live wire: jittery, cocky, sarcastic. They head straight for the deejay booth where Jellybean is mixing into the new David Bowie single, "Let's Dance."

"It's a good night," says Jellybean. When a deejay feels each segue pumping the crowd, he knows it's all working—he's at one with the crowd, he's hot. "It's nights like this that I feel I could play anything and they'd still go crazy. Sometimes, it's like an endless peak."

Baker looks out through the clown's gaping mouth and sees three Buggas dancing. Two years ago, long before Baker arrived, the Buggas ruled the Fun House. They brought a new style: gym shorts, t-shirts cut off at the midriff, sweat-bands. The look was a reaction against the let's-dress-up-and-hustle craze that swept through New York in the '70s. The Buggas hate the hustle, which they think is too formal, too bourgeois, too social, and too lame. According to some Fun House regulars, the Buggas prefer to take a lot of drugs (mostly speed) and just...bug out. They usually stand in front of the mirrors, slowly accelerating until they are functioning at the dance world equivalent of Mach-5. The dance is fairly simple, a cross between the Monkey and running in place. The outer limbs are a furious, windmilling blur, while the upper torso and head remains remarkably stationary. They can perform this ritual facing the mirrors for hours. If a hair falls out-of-place, a hand will move up and correct the problem, while the rest of the body continues bugging.

Some people here still respect the Buggas, but their time has probably come and gone. They used to control the back stage, but the Juice Crew elbowed them out of that prestigious spot last year. The Buggas are getting a little too old (over 20) and a little too burnt-out.

"There are a few people here," observes Jellybean, "who seem to be trapped in a strange time warp."

Sunday 2:30 a.m.

For the past three hours, the Juice Crew has been underneath the balcony, trading gossip, warming up, practicing a few routines.

Now, with the first big peak coming fast, they gather on the back stage. Everyone is present: Mama Juice, Berico, Brown Sugar, Brian, Chino, Starstruck, Crazy Evette, Coco, Stepsaver, and, unexpectedly, Tony, who is also known as White Lightning.

Although widely considered the best dancer in the crew, Tony has not been at the Fun House in months. Instead, he has been frequenting other clubs like Paradise Garage and The Loft.

"I love the Fun House," he says. "It's like a home away from home. But I'm looking for a new club. I've been to practically all the clubs, and I can tell you none of them are like this place. How would I describe this place? Weird. I think a lot of insecure people come here. I don't know why they dance in front of mirrors. I guess they get off on seeing themsevles dance. It gets rid of their tensions. Believe me, there's a lot of tense people at the Fun House."

Tony is 19. He dropped out of high school and works as a bookkeeper for the American Blueprint Company on47th Street. He has short-cropped hair with a long tail in back. He wears grey baggies, gray sweatshirt, and gray suede sneakers. Many people mistake him for Spanish, but he's Irish and Italian. He lives with his sister's family in Bensonhurst.

The B-boys have taken over the back stage. Brian and Chino take turns spinning of their shoulders, their back, their heads. Chino puts a glove on, leaps in the air, lands on one hand, and spins around several times. A large crowd gathers. Mister Freeze, a member of the Rock Steady Crew and a featured performer in the recent movie Flashdance, is spotted in the crowd. Mister Freeze is a master of a robotic, mimelike dance known as Electric Boogie. He is coaxed onstage, given plenty of room and all the solo time he wants. Later, however, when an unknown breaker enters the circle and performs a ducklike walk, Mama Juice and her girlfriends pounce on the hapless victim, mercilessly imitating his awkward, uncreative moves. This safeguards against medicore dancers taking over the stage.

Tony decides to check out the competition in the rest of the club and wanders off to the main floor. "Hip Hop, Be Bop" by Man Parrish is playing and the song provokes a gutteral doglike barking from all corners of the room. "Wooff! Wooff! Wooff!" Two glassy-eyed friends meet on the floor. The music is too loud to talk over, but the intensity and duration of their barking signals they are having a good time. Tony moves to the center of the floor and executes a few spins. He is suddenly aware of two Spanish kids staring at him. They are wearing Lees, Garrison belts, and chains galore. The tall one wears a Civil War cap with crossed rifles on the front.

"Check this white boy out," says the one with the cap. Tony has a very distinctive style that incorporates elements of modern jazz and classical ballet. He has gotten into many fights after hearing the word "fag" whispered in his direction.

"You want to check this white boy out?" he says. "You do your thing, and I'll do mine." A circle forms around them. The one with the hat looks at the crowd, smirks, and crosses his arms on his chest. He waves a hand in Tony's face indicating "No thanks."

"Listen," says Tony, his voice tense. "Either we throw down dancing or we throw down fighting."

"Ohh," says the short one. "That's a call."

"Yeah, I'm calling," says Tony.

"You think you're bad, don't choo?" he says cooly.

"I *know* I'm bad," answers Tony.

The one with the cap moves to the center of the circle and starts to dance. His style is a mixture of freestyle and B-boy. He executes a rapid succession of choreographed steps, spins, and backbends. "He's good," Tony says later, "but not good enough." Just as the Spanish kid is losing energy, "Time Warp" by Eddy Grant comes on. It just happens to be Tony's favorite song. Tony spins to the center of the circle, dips his hands down and throws an imaginary substance into his opponent's face. The crowd applauds.

"Go, Tony, go!" shouts a friend.

Tony glides effortlessly across the floor. He kicks out, back bends, and throws his torso in the direction of the Spanish kids, who are already looking humiliated. Tony has burned the guy with the cap.

When Tony finally stops, there's a line of sweat running down his forehead. "Before you can shoot someone down," he says, "you have to know what you can do."

Sunday 4:55 a.m.

Coco can't believe her eyes. She's seen some gorgeous guys at the Fun House, but this one is really something. Too bad no one in the Juice Crew knows who he is. He's tall, dark-skinned, muscular, and has a mescaline smile tugging at the corners of his mouth. He steps in the center of the circle, whips off his t-shirt and starts gyrating. The girls go wild. He pulls the drawstring on his baggies, briefly lowers his pants, and reveals a blue G-string.

"Ohhh gawd," says Coco. "I don't believe it."

A girl enters the circle. She shyly approaches the dancer, sticks a dollar bill down his pants, and runs away. The crowd roars.

"I feel like going in," says Coco.

"Go ahead, go ahead," says Mama Juice.

Coco grabs a dollar bill, sticks it between her teeth and moves into the circle. She is tall and slender and wears Chinese slippers, semi-transparent harem pants, and a blue t-shirt rolled up her torso. Her dancing is sinuous, magically erotic. She moves in front of the dancer and spreads her legs. She expects him to dive headfirst under her—a favorite move at the Fun House. Instead, he comes up behind her, drops his baggies, and starts bumping his pelvis against her hips. Coco covers her eyes and feigns dismay. The dollar bill is still clasped between her teeth. She waves her hands helplessly over her head. He moves under her and lifts her with his pelvis. They move slowly and methodically. The dance is innocent yet sexy but not aggressive and raunchy. When they leave the circle, they get the biggest applause of the night.

"I'm so embarrassed," laughs Coco while hiding her face.

Sunday 6:05 a.m.

Three quarters of the dancers have left. Others are slumped on the floor, lying on couches, or sitting with their backs against the wall. Only the hardcore dancers are left. The Juice Crew has scattered to all corners of the floor. Jellybean mixes a live version of "Sex Machine" by James Brown. Brian and Chino leap on the back stage and start Brooklyn Rocking (a dance known as "Up-Rock" or "Top-Rock" to those in the Bronx who give credit for its creation to the legendary Phase 2 and his crew.) They bend their knees, touch the floor, jump up and deliver fake karate blows to each other. Sometimes they jump up and pretend to have a knife or a gun. An Italian kid from the center stage happens to be standing next to them. He thinks they're really fighting and takes a swing at Chino. Three bouncers run over to the stage, grab the Italian kid, and lead him away. Brain and Chino keep dancing.

Sunday 8:30 a.m.

The music stops. The crowd boos. "Fuck it, fuck it, fuck it," screams one dancer. Six scavengers are crawling across the floor of the balcony, picking up foil wrappers, and checking them for drugs. The wrappers are the trash left by users of cocaine, angel dust, speed, or mescaline. A dozen bouncers form a chain and gently prod the dancers out the door, like cowhands driving a herd of weary cattle. The dancers collect on the front steps. They look sleepy, but are reluctant to leave.

"The Juice Crew is very close," says Tony while standing on the steps and waiting for his friends. "We don't have much, but what we have, we share amongst each other and make the bests of it. We go to each other's houses and sleep over. We trust each other. This may sound funny, but I consider us actors and actresses in a whole new way. So much comes out when we're dancing—little personality things and ideas we have. After a night of dancing, every problem I have is gone—erased from my mind.

The Juice Crew leaves together. They are disappointed to find it raining outside. If the weather were better, they would go to Washington Square Park and dance for several more hours. Instead, they'll have breakfast and go home.

\

The Pied Piper of Hip Hop

Never one to let Black History Month slip by without commemoration, Afrika Bambaataa held his third annual party celebrating the occasion of February 25, 1982. As usual, the festivities were staged at the Bronx River Community Center, a squat, fortress-like structure located in the heart of the southeast Bronx. An impressive list of the most famous rappers, DJs and MC groups in the Bronx, including Kool Herc, Grandmaster Flash, the Treacherous Three, Grandwizzard Theodore, and the Cold Crush Brothers, had promised to drop by and perform. The concert was free and, like most rap music extravaganzas, it was expected to be a loose, informal, and unpredictable affair. For this reason, few audience members would have been surprised if many of the advertised performers failed to appear—which, in fact, is exactly what happened.

Around noon, a sound system was installed in the center's gymnasium and a few hours later dance-music began blasting out of a pair of five-foot speaker columns. Almost immediately, a smattering of young black males began drifting into the gym, most of whom lounged against the back wall and stared at the stage.

Finally, the rapping segment of the show began when Bizzy Bee Starsky, the rap equivalent of a lead-off batter, grabbed the microphone and cut a wide swath through the crowd as he pranced across the stage. The dancers, many of whom were dressed in hoodies, leather bomber jackets, basketball sneakers, and jeans, pressed closer to the stage.

"Everybody who likes sex throw your hands in the air!" screamed Bizzy Bee. The audience threw up its hands and roared in approval. With his double-knit slacks and clunky black shoes and impeccable grooming, Bizzy looked a bit out-of-place here, but he was obviously a crowd favorite. Bizzy Bee had already won top-awards for solo rapping two years in a row at the famous Harlem

World showdowns. He was among one of the first rappers in the Bronx, and he'd already had years of experience pumping up crowds.

"What's the name of this nation?!!" shouted Bizzy Bee, his wiry body quivering with energy. "Zulu!! Zulu!!" chanted the crowd. "And who's gonna get on down?!" asked Bizzy with a smile.

"Bambaataa!! Bambaataa!!"

Li'l Vietnam

Afrika Bambaataa, founder and number one DJ of the mighty Zulu Nation, grew up at the Bronx River Project, which is situated near the intersection of the Cross Bronx and Bronx River expressways and looks like every other low-income housing project in the city, a cluster of unadorned, 15-story brick buildings circling two small playgrounds. Unlike the nearby South Bronx, the neighborhood survived the '60s relatively intact with few buildings abandoned. The surrounding community is filled with row after row of identical, two-story brick houses, most of which have tiny concrete yards, framed by cast-iron fences. It looks quiet here but this neighborhood once had a reputation for violence that was unequaled in New York.

Bronx River Projects

It all started in 1968 at the nearby Bronxdale Project when seven incorrigible teenagers, who were terrorizing playgrounds, robbing bus drivers, and wreaking havoc throughout the southeast Bronx, began calling themselves the Savage Seven. In imitation of Hell's Angels, they began wearing Levi jackets with a gang-like insignia emblazoned on the back. Before long, others wanted to join and the name had to be changed to the Black Spades. The group was then an official street gang, one of the first to appear since the late

'50s, when the widespread use of heroin demolished what was left of the original gangs.

Almost immediately, gangs modeled after the Black Spade appeared at every project in the Bronx, all wearing the same uniform: jeans, Levi jackets, garrison belts, black engineer boots. At first, teenagers joined because they liked the style and because it was fun to drift around the city like a pack of wolves. Later on, it became necessary to join in order to survive. Without a gang affiliation, a young boy was vulnerable to beatings, robbery, and general day-to-day harassment. However, as soon as he started flying colors, everyone knew he couldn't be bullied without arousing the wrath of several hundred well-armed compatriots.

A division of Black Spades was founded at Bronx River Project in 1969 and Bambaataa, then a junior high school student, immediately became a member. But he was far from being a typical one; while other gang members were playing basketball or hanging out on street corners, he was scouring record bins for obscure R&B recordings.

"Bam was never interested in sports. As long as I've known him, he's always been the music man," says Jay McGluery, who grew up at Bronx River with Bambaataa. "His mother is a nurse and she was constantly on the go, so we always went to his house to party. He had every record you could want to hear, including a lot of rock albums. James Brown and Sly and the Family Stone was his favorites."

Bambaataa was also more attuned to politics than most of his fellow gang members, many of whom reportedly understood only three concepts: crush, kill and destroy. When he was 12, Bambaataa had already begun hanging out at the Black Panther Information Center on Boston Road. His political leanings were encouraged by the appearance of songs like "Say It Loud, I'm

Black and I'm Proud" by James Brown and "Stand" by Sly and the Family Stone.

However, like many gang members, Bambaataa had a reckless, unpredictable streak. McGluery recalls the time they were playing war games and he took refuge in one of the project's apartment buildings. Bambaataa poured gasoline on the sidewalk in front of the building, lit it, and announced he was holding everyone hostage. That same summer he convinced his friends to buy target bows and arrows so they could hunt rabbits on the banks of the Bronx River. "Bam was always a leader,": says McGluery. "He was always full of crazy ideas."

It wasn't long before the war games ended, however, and the real wars began.

It seemed natural for the street gangs to turn against the local heroin dealers. After all, drugs had destroyed the previous gangs and were certainly capable of having a similar effect on them. "Getting rid of the pushers caused great problems for us because we grew up knowing most of them," says McGluery. "Yet they was causin' great harm in the community, so we came to the conclusion that gang members from other projects would do the work. We just had to point them out and that night they might get a good beating." Many dealers quickly relocated to different parts of the city. The more difficult cases were often found thrown off a roof or shot to death. The Royal Charmers went so far as to erect a paint-splattered sheet across 173rd Street that read: "No junkies allowed after 10 o'clock."

The number of gangs in the Bronx kept growing through the summer in 1971, but this development went unnoticed until Stevenson High School opened its doors in September. Located in the North Bronx, Stevenson had been a predominantly white school that was now receiving busloads of blacks and Hispanics from the South Bronx. The first day was quiet. The second day a few of the gang members decided to wear their colors to school. The third day it was apparent that almost the entire male population belonged to one gang or another. Finding themselves outnumbered, a variety of white gangs merged into a single gang called the Ministers. Fights between the Black Spades and the Ministers soon became a daily event and would continue for the next two years.

Fortunately, a conclusive battle between the two groups was never fought. A few major rumbles were arranged but the warlords on each side, but whenever the Black Spades boarded a bus headed uptown, it would be surrounded by squad cars long before it could even reach the Minister's turf. Typically, the windows of the bus would fly open and a shower of chains, knives, bats, and zip guns would hit the pavement. On June 27,1973, a brief battle was broken up by the police in front of P.S. 127 on Castle Hill Avenue, resulting in the arrest of 18 Black Spades. The police, almost entirely white at the time, were constantly being accused of racism, a charge that might have had some foundation considering newspaper stories from this time indicate that white gang members were seldom arrested.

As the gangs of the south and southeast Bronx grew progressively violent and uncontrollable, they eventually began to turn on each other, a development that produced the bloodiest confrontations. One feud between the Black Spades and the Seven Crowns lasted for 92 days, during which time the Bronx River Project was constantly peppered with gunfire from passing cars. Shoot-outs became so common that the residents started calling it "Lil' Vietnam."

I was into street gang violence," admits Bambaataa. "That was all part of growing up in the southeast Bronx." However, that's about all he'll say on the subject. "I don't really be speaking on that stuff because its negative," he explains. "The Black Spades was also helping out in the community, raising money for sickle cell anemia and gettin' people to register to vote."

"He was not what I would call gung-ho," adds McGluery, who became warlord of the Bronx River division before quitting to join the Marines. "Bam was more like a supervisor. There were so many different gangs and he knew at least five members in every one. And any time there was a conflict, he would try and straighten it out. He was into communications."

Gang activity probably peaked in 1973, when there were an estimated 315 gangs in the city with 19,503 claimed members. The Black Spades was by far the largest and most feared, with divisions in almost every precinct. However, by 1974, the Black Spades began to disintegrate. "Girls got tired of the gangs first," says Bambaataa. "They wanted to raise families and they'd seen too many people dyin'. Some gangs got into drugs. Others got wiped out—by the police or other gangs."

After many of the original Black Spades were killed, jailed or dropped out of the gang, Bambaataa took on an increasingly influential role. His affiliation continued until January 10, 1975, when his best friend, Soulski, was shot and killed by two policemen on Pelham Parkway. Bambaataa insists the shooting was nothing short of an assassination carried out during a police crackdown on gang activity. He keeps a copy of his friend's death certificate in his bedroom. "He got shot in about nine different places," says Bambaataa. "The back, the stomach, the face. At first I wanted to go to war with the police but we really couldn't win. The Amsterdam News calmed everybody down and told us to fight through the system. It went to trial but the cops never got convicted."

For over five years the Bronx had lived in constant terror of street gangs.Suddenly, in 1975, they disappeared almost as quickly as they'd arrived. This happened because something better came along to take their place. That something was hip hop.

Birth of the New Cool

On August 11, 1973, Kool Herc and Coke La Rock had hosted a birthday party for Herc's sister Cindy in the recreation room at 1520 Sedgwick Avenue. Within two years, the style they created, the records they played, the dances they helped inspire, the way they talked, would transform the Bronx with a whole new style. Suddenly, the DJ. an independent entrepreneur armed with a portable sound system and extensive record collection emerged as a new culture hero and tribal leader. In Bambaataa's neighborhood, the first DJ with two turntables, a mixer, and a cult following was Kool Dee, whose repertoire consisted primarily of the same disco hits aired on black-oriented radio stations.

"We began to hear about this DJ in the West Bronx who was playing a whole new sound," says Bambaataa. "At first I didn't like it, because I sided with Kool Dee. But Herc's music was more funky than Kool Dee's, so I switched."

Herc had moved to New York from Kingston in 1967 and his approach was patterned after the great Jamaican DJs, who'd developed a singular style, building huge speaker systems on flatbed trucks that could travel around the country putting on shows anywhere, anytime. Herc knew the value in having the most powerful equipment that could produce the loudest and cleanest sounds. By the early '60s, Jamaican DJs had also developed a style of talking over instrumentals known as "toasting." Reggae singles were often pressed with a dub side, a musical track without a vocal, so DJs could fill in with their own impromptu lyrics. In 1973, Herc had plenty of dub reggae records but he couldn't play any of them because his audience wouldn't accept reggae. So he played played the funkiest disco records he could find, many with a Latin flavor. "Apache" by the Incredible Bongo Band quickly became one of his many signature songs. Written by Jerry Lordan and originally released by a British guitar band called The Shadows in 1960, it had been covered by numerous acts, including The Ventures. In 1973, the Incredible Bongo Band removed the Indian drum beat dominating the previous versions and replaced it with a West Indian congo beat. Herc turned the song into the Bronx national anthem.

Herc was the first DJ to buy records just for the breaks, the 15-second instrumental when the band was at its funkiest, and he always had to have two copies, so he could extend those breaks for as long as he wanted. Coke La Rock did most of the talking at first. "Hotel, motel, you don't tell, I won't tell," was the sort of stuff that popped into Coke's head while he was improving on the mic, but his favorite—and most-used—line was: "You rock and you don't stop." Eventually Herc also began developing a unique vocal style, with lines like, "Rock on, my mellow, this is the joint." Talking on the microphone during the party was something most people found intimidating at first. But once you saw the results it could produce on the crowd if you did it right, "rapping" became everyone's favorite past-time. The best dancers would wait for the best breaks and go wild. Herc referred to them as his "b-boys." The Nigger Twins may have been the best and were heavily influenced by James Brown; they learned most of his steps before inventing their own. But first came Sa-sa, who perfected a drop still known in Bronx today as "The Sa-sa Drop."

Once Herc got popular, his parties moved to the Heavalo, the Twilight Zone, and the Executive Playhouse, and his crowd came with him. "If you was at one of Herc's parties, it was something big, something you'd go home and brag about," recalled Grandmixer DST. "When 'Apache' came on, everybody would form a circle and the b-boys would go into the center. At first, the dances were simple. Then some guy dropped to the floor and began to spin around. Everybody said, 'wow' and went home and tried to come back with something better. At first, you'd be in the center for a half minute, then one minute, then two minutes. People started puttin' perfection into the dance."

Within a few months, 'breaking' evolved into a highly acrobatic, ritualized contest that, to some extent, replaced fighting as a major outlet for aggression. Graffiti master Phase 2 remembers the Up-Rock style as having originated with him and his friends, all of whom were original Herc b-boys. Up-rocking looked exactly like fighting to most outsiders. Breaking, on the other hand, usually involved dropping to the floor and spinning in some form.

Meanwhile, at Stevenson High, Bambaataa had formed a small social group called The Zulus, inspired by a recent release of a feature film on the tribe. (The original Bambaataa was a Zulu chief at the turn of the century. Translated into English the word means "affectionate leader.") The Zulus became an extension of Herc's b-boy style. They were a more sophisticated version of the Black Spades, a gang into music and dance instead of violence. When Bambaataa graduated in December 1975, his mother bought him a sound system. His first official performance as a DJ was at the Bronx River Community Center on November 12, 1976.

By this time, the new dances were were spreading all over the Bronx and the DJs began battling each other. While this was considerably less dangerous than a gang fight, it did capture the excitement of a major confrontation. Two DJs, each representing his own neighborhood or musical style, would meet at a junior high gym or public park and engage in a bloodless battle, which often consisted of both playing at the same time with both systems cranked to maximum volume. This was the sort of competition

Herc never lost, since his system towered over everyone else's at the time. "There was a lot of confusion going on at the time," laughs Bambaataa. "If you out-blasted the other DJ, he'd get mad, cut off his system, and leave."

There were also less honorable methods of competing, methods Kool Herc remembers well. "If Bam and I had a battle, we knew it was just a gimmick to attract people," he says. "But the Zulus would take it to heart and start pulling plugs. Bam is not to be blamed for that," Herc adds quickly. "He ain't that type of person. Anybody who picks up the wax is a friend in my heart, but Bam is the only DJ I really respect because he always plays music I never heard before."

During one legendary battle against Disco King Mario, Bambaataa opened his set with the theme song from the Andy Griffith show, taped off his television set. He mixed into a rocking drum beat, followed it with the Munsters' theme song and quickly changed gears with "I Got the Feeling," by James Brown. His knack for bugging out the audience with unexpected segues earned him the title, "Master of Records."

There is much more to Bambaataa's mystique than a few novelty records, however. For many troubled kids he provides a hip yet strongly moral and positive role model. "Bam tells them not to drink, smoke or take drugs, and to stay in school until they get a diploma," says McGluery. "He's a Black Muslim and when he talks to the kids, you can feel the vibrations from the Muslims coming through." When asked what the Zulu Nation is all about, Bambaataa simply replies: "It's about survival, economics, and keeping our people moving on."

DST remembers the first time he discovered the Zulus. "My friends and I were checking out all the dance parties," he says. "We heard about his guy Bambaataa and went to P.S. 123 to see him. I remember seeing all these b-boys and thinking, 'yeah, they got them over here too.' I started going to more of Bam's parties and was invited to join up. It wasn't like being in the Black Spades. The Spades were heartless lunatics. The Zulu Nation was about bringing peace. Force was only used if necessary. Bam had a good idea. He brought people together from all parts of the Bronx. It was one of the main factors to end the warfare."

In 1977 the ranks of the Zulu Nation were spreading into other boroughs as well. Becoming a Zulu wasn't difficult, all you had to do was show up at the right parties and express an interest in joining. What was remarkable, however, was the number of kids seeking application, a number Bambaataa says he can no longer estimate, but one that undoubtedly runs into the thousands. "Bam has some kind of gift with the kids," says McGluery. "I don't think even he knows how the Zulus got so big." "A lot of people liked our style," says Bambaataa with his usual understatement.

Not only do they like his style, the Zulus exhibit a fierce loyalty to their leader. "He is the music," says Cholly Rock, an original Zulu b-boy who is often credited with spreading break dancing into Manhattan. When Cholly Rock tries to explain Bambaataa's role, he hesitates as if what he wants to say is too complicated to put into words. "He makes it all come together," he says finally.

In 1977, a young DJ in the South Bronx named Grandmaster Flash began revolutionizing Herc's DJ style. Like most, Flash had started as a b-boy, but after he hurt his back doing a flip, he switched to DJing. He wired his miniature system to a street light in Echo Park and provided free concerts on the weekends. He taught himself how to extend breaks without dropping a single beat. He called it "the merry-go-round." He also learned how to pinpoint the exact spot on the groove he needed to drop his needle, a technique he called "the clock method." Flash created the art of live musical collage. His equipment was stored at Mean

Gene's house, and Gene had a little brother named Theodore who was inspired by Flash. Rehearsing one day, Theodore invented a technique for creating percussive sounds and beats by rapidly moving the record forward and back while keeping the needle in the groove. It would become known as "scratching." Then Flash discovered how to program a beat machine, and introduced "The Beat Box" as a major part of his shows. Simultaneously, Flash created the best MC group in the Bronx. Cowboy came first, joined soon by Melle Mel. It was Mel who created the hardest possible attack with his rapping style, and also began experimenting with lyrics that went way beyond nursery rhymes and ego-boasts.

"A child is born with no state of mind, blind to the ways of mankind. God's smiling on you but he's frowning too, 'cause only God knows what you'll go through," says Mel on his first record, "Super Rappin.'"

Relying on inventive use of slang, the staccato effect of short words and strong syllables, and unexpected internal rhymes, the Furious Five began creating elaborate rap routines, intricately weaving their voices through a musical track mixed by Flash. They would trade solos, chant, and even, sometimes, sing harmony. The result was dazzling. It was a vocal style immediately imitated by every other MC group, and one that shifted the attention away from the DJ and onto the new stars, the rappers. Theadore and Mean Gene formed their own group, one that included Bizzy Bee, and called themselves the L Brothers. Grandmaster Caz had also emerged as a force; he was invited into the Cold Crush Brothers by their DJs Charlie Chase and Tony Tone. Bambaata began developing a number of rap groups, including the Soul Sonic Force, the Cosmic Force, and the Jazzy Five. However, he remembers the best battles taking place at the time between Flash and the Furious Five versus Breakout and the Funky Four (later known as the Funky Four Plus 1.) Flash had been on top ever since the day he beat Herc in a battle (using Herc's signature records against him), but the Funky Four became the first group to purchase mic stands and teach themselves organized dance routines. "The Furious Five and Funky Four was battling for that number one spot," recalls Bambaataa. "Both groups was doin' flips on stages and settin' off smoke bombs."

For over five years the b-boys, rappers, DJs, and graffiti writers of the Bronx continued to expand and develop their unique artistic vision is almost complete isolation from the rest of the world. Until 1979, little attempt was made to spread the subculture, which didn't really even have a name, at least not a name widely used inside the culture itself. The words "hip hop" eventually developed out of an improv Cowboy came up with during a going-away party for a relative who'd joined the service and was being posted overseas. But even that term was only used by a handful of people in 1979 and it had never appeared in print.

When the Fatback Band released "King Tim III," a few of the original MC groups were inspired to put out a record of their own. (For years, rap had only been transmitted through live recordings on cassette tape, which were noisily displayed via the ghetto blasters carried by every self-respecting hip hopper.) The first rap record to come out of the New York area was "Rapper's Delight" by the Sugarhill Gang, which unexpectedly sold two million copies, launched a new independent label, created a vast audience for rap around the country (and unleashed a mad scramble of MC groups looking for recording contracts). The song's success must have stung the real Bronx rap groups, however, since the Sugarhill Gang were basically amateurs, who soft, disco style carried none of the authority of a Melle Mel. Even worse, the best lines in the song were all stolen from Grandmaster Caz. Almost every b-boy in the Bronx knew those rhymes about Superman and Lois Lane were his.

The major labels warily kept their distance and a number of small independent companies began producing rap records. Bambaataa visited several, dropping off tapes, and received only minor encouragement. Finally, in 1980, he succeeded in obtaining a deal with Paul Winley's struggling label. In November, he recorded two 12-inch versions of "Zulu Throwdown," one with Cosmic Force and the other with the Soul Sonic Force. When the first single was released, however, Bambaataa discovered Winley had added instruments without even consulting him. "It was crazy," says Bam. "I recorded the songs to just drums. When the record came out, Winley added a bass and some crazy guitar music. Then when it came time to get paid, he started jivin' us. A lot of groups at the time weren't business-wise and didn't know about contracts or royalties. We just wanted to get a record out."

Instead of moving forward, Bambaataa felt he was losing ground. He hated his own record and knew he wasn't getting the recognition he deserved as one of the top DJs of hip hop. The precariousness of the situation was all the more evident by what had happened to Kool Herc, who was now working at a record store in the South Bronx. Herc's slide from power, which began after the battle with Flash, ended one night at the Executive Playhouse, when he stepped in to break up a fight. Coke La Rock, who was also Herc's enforcer since he carried a gun (every DJ needed an enforcer to protect the valuable equipment), had gone home momentarily to use his bathroom (his apartment was right around the corner), but when Coke got back seconds later, Herc had already been transported to the hospital.

"I knew one of the guys involved," recalls Herc. "But one of his friends thought I was messin' with him. He stabbed me three times. After that the door was open. How do you think people feel about comin' to a party when the host gets stabbed? Papa couldn't find no good ranch anymore so his herd scattered."

Coke wanted to go hunting for the perpetrator immediately, but Herc's dad made him give up his gun for 24-hours. Coke broke into tears on the spot, begged him to ask for anything but that, but eventually Coke handed over his gun for the night. The culprit was moved back down south, far from the Bronx, and although Coke would spend several days searching for him with the aim of putting a bullet in his head, eventually Coke realized he probably needed to get out of hip hop before he killed somebody or somebody killed him.

In 1981, Bambaataa had just established a relationship with a fledgling label called Tommy Boy Records when he received a phone call from graffiti artist Fred Brathwaite (Fab Five Freddy), who was about to co-curate a graffiti exhibit at the newly opened Mudd Club Gallery. Brathwaite asked Bambaataa to perform at the opening and he readily accepted the invitation. It was his first contact with the downtown music scene and Bambaataa was greatly impressed, not only by the enthusiasm and energy of the crowd, but by their appreciative response to "Zulu Nation Throwdown." "They thought is was a classic," says Bambaataa incredulously. "After that, I started to like it too."

"Bambaataa is a smart guy," says Brathwaite, who was one of the first graffiti artists to mingle with the East Village art scene, hanging out at Club 57 and exhibiting at alternative spaces like P.S. 1. "After the Mudd Club, he knew just what to do. The rest is history."

What Bambaataa did was to go into the studio and immediately begin work on a new record, one that would appeal to the new wave crowd as well as the hip hoppers. He raided musical fragments from sources he felt were appreciated by both groups: Kraftwerk, the film "The Good, the Bad and the Ugly," and Captain Sky. With the help of producers Tom Silverman and Arthur Baker, keyboardist John Robie, and a Roland TR 808 drum computer, Bambaataa created an eerie yet throbbingly funky musical track. He encourage Soul Sonic Force to come up with a new style of rap to augment the music. The result, invented by GLOBE, discarded the aggressive hard style and replaced it with one that extended notes into a chant before abruptly cutting them off. It had none of Melle Mel's impact, but it was a peculiar technique that well-suited the song.

The final result, titled "Planet Rock," was released in May 1982, and, according to Billboard, the record was "an instant club and retail hit of formidable size, shipping near-gold on release." Bambaataa suddenly found himself catapulted into national recognition.
"One thing we like to stress," says Bambaataa, who has just returned from a whirlwind tour of Florida and South Carolina. "Success will not make us big-headed. Some people say, 'How does it feel to be a star?' We don't look at ourselves as stars. 'Cause stars fall. We want to be like the moon and stay put. We still go to the same places we always went and we still talk to everybody, whether they are young or old. We wish everybody the best. We paid our dues and we'll reach down and pull others up with us. We want to keep our money in the community." In his many snapshots from the '60s, Bambaataa looks young, lean and angry, his eyebrows fused in a permanent scowl of disapproval. Today, however, the angry young man has put on weight and mellowed considerably. He projects a guarded, reserved aura that is sometimes shattered by a smile so friendly it disarms and infects everyone around him. As soon as "Planet Rock" took off, he went out and celebrated by getting a mohawk haircut. "In the future, I just hope all my groups keep piping," he explains. "See, George Clinton took the music of James Brown and Sly and the Family Stone and made a whole funk empire out of it. That's what I'm trying to do with rap."

Who knows? In another five years, hip hop could be considered the most significant artistic achievement of the decade. There are certainly signs that its influence is on the rise. For example, in a recent issue of Flash Art magazine, Diego Cortez, an influential freelance curator, said: "The rap and breaking phenomenon is just starting to have an effect on the official culture in New York and elsewhere, and I think that this will be clear in the next couple years, this influence as the New York image, music and gesture. I think the work should be looked at as a highly sophisticated art form which is the image of New York. It's definitely the soul of the underground scene at the moment."

Even more recent was Malcolm McLaren's keynote address at the 1982 New Music Seminar in New York. The creator of the Sex Pistols surprised his audience by devoting most of his speech to rap music. "Planet Rock, is the most rootsy music around," said McLaren, "the only music that's coming out of New York City which has tapped and directly related to that guy with the ghetto blaster. The record is like an adventure story; it's like that guy walking down the street. And, if Elvis Presley was that in the '50s, then Afrika Bambaataa is that for the '80s....This music has a magical air about it because it's not trapped by the preconditioning and evaluation of what a pop record has to be."

Few New York subcultures in the past decade have been so relentlessly creative as the one that has given us rap music, graffiti writing, and break dancing, perhaps the first youth culture to put its highest premium on individual imagination and innovation. It isn't enough for a DJ to merely spin records, he has to amaze his audience with a display of turntable pyrotechnics. It isn't enough for a graffiti writer to spray his name, he has to devout hours to create a mural that will cover an entire subway car. It isn't enough for a break dancer to do a flip, he has to learn to spin like a top while doing a headstand.

If subcultures are the experimental laboratory where society tests new cultural concepts, then hip hop represents the most imaginative leap forward since the '60s. And like the counterculture of the '60s, hip hop has the capacity to infiltrate and subvert the mass media culture, energizing it with a fresh supply of symbols, myths, and values. Certainly the potential is there and the outcome now depends largely on the artists like Bambaataa, who are finally enjoying a measure of success. Will they rise to the occasion, hold on to their principles, and spread the new hip hop sensibility around the globe? I think so.

Is the Art World Ready for Graffiti?

They started as outlaws, invading the subway yards by night, armed with fists full of magic markers and sacks full of spray paint. More than a decade later, the graffiti writers, as they call themselves, are still waging a guerrilla war against the Metropolitan Transit Association (MTA), which spends millions of dollars each year to erase their fanciful handiwork. Lately, though, the more ambitious writers have acquired a new, above ground cachet, and a new audience for their efforts. With the encouragement of some influential gallery owners and collectors, the subway scrawlers are making a serious bid to be accepted into the art world.

On April 9, 1981, an exhibit of their paintings, "Beyond Words," opens at the Mudd Club gallery; graffiti writers also have participated in four New York alternative-space exhibitions in the last six months. Sam Esses, a private collector, recently announced plans for a European tour of 47 graffiti paintings, and Art Letter, a newsletter for dealers and collectors, devoted a third of its February issue to describing recent advances on the graffiti frontier. "I think they (the writers) are producing some of the best work by young artists today," says Leo Castelli, the Soho gallery owner who represents Jasper Johns, Roy Lichtenstein, Andy Warhol and Claes Oldenburg. "They have the talent to make it in the art world; all they need is the opportunity."

The notion of subway graffiti as art was first entertained in the early '70s: Richard Goldstein wrote a critical evaluation of graffiti in New York magazine, and Norman Mailer and Jon Naar published a book called "The Faith of Graffiti," which provoked sneers from some of the writers.

Then, in 1973, a group called the United Graffiti Artists—which included some of the hottest writers in New York—put on an exhibit at the now-defunct Razor Gallery. For the first time, writers were brought off the streets, given canvas and paint, and encouraged to create sellable works of art. Although the opening was widely covered, the paintings didn't sell well and public interest in the project soon fizzled.

"The problem with those writers is they promised never to paint the trains again," says Fred, who belongs to a "The Fabulous Five," a graffiti group immortalized in the recent Blondie hit "Rapture." Like many of his peers, Fred believes he must stay in touch with real graffiti—by returning to subway yards—in order to avoid "selling out the art." Futura 2000, another prominent writer, also insists that "painting the trains is what gives our work credibility. They were trying to create a graffiti elite, which is something we aren't interested in." But the new graffiti flowering as another impulse. Says Futura matter-of-factly: "Our work has gotten much better."

Patti Astor and Fred Brathwaite on the set of Wild Style; publicity photo.

Observers confirm that the quality of work has improved dramatically in the past year, a development which may have been helped, at least in part, to Sam Esses, who provided studio space last spring for fledgling writers to refine their skills.

Esses' route to the writers was circuitous. In 1979, a Swiss photographer took pictures of a graffiti mural on a handball court on the lower East Side, painted by Fred and Lee, the founder of the Fabulous Five. The pictures eventually landed on the desk of an Italian art dealer named Claudio Bruni, who was sufficiently impressed with the mural to make an effort to find the artists who created it. Because the graffiti community is tight-knit—and because Fred and Lee are well-known and highly respected—he had no trouble. Bruni gave them canvas to paint on and took the results back to Rome, where the paintings sold for $1,000 each.

Esses, a burly, outspoken collector from New Jersey who now lives on Park Avenue, became aware of a growing European interest in graffiti through contacts with Bruni. When he discovered that his 15-year-old daughter knew some of the writers, he decided to make contact.

Esses admits that he is an unlikely candidate to play a key role in the introduction of graffiti to the "straight" art world; his own taste, he concedes, tends more towards trompe l'oeil. "I don't know why, but I decided to rent a studio to see if I could preserve some of the work that was being created on the trains. I found an empty studio on the upper East Side and stocked it with supplies." Word soon spread through the graffiti grapevine, and the best writers from all over the city quickly materialized on Esses' doorstep. A highly competitive atmosphere developed, and over the next couple of months some of the graffiti began showing signs of rapid improvement.

According to Esses, the results began to show up last summer on the trains. The crude name writing (called "tagging") was being replaced by more sophisticated full-car murals (called "masterpieces") Masterpieces had been done before, but they now seemed more elaborate, filled with cityscapes, cartoon characters and complex color fields. The newer work, in fact, resembles the massive Pop paintings of the '60s.

Cover of a catalog for an Italian show produced by Claudio Bruni featuring Fab Five Freddy and Lee Quinones, collection of Steven Hager.

Writers have become so adept at manipulating spray paint that they can blend colors effortlessly, sometimes spraying two cans at once. In one favorite technique, a writer starts with a dark color at the bottom of a train which slowly blends to a lighter color at the top; the result, something akin to a psychedelic sunset, is called a "fade." Some murals even make reference to art history; in homage to Andy Warhol, Fred recently painted a train with gigantic Campbell soup cans, labeled Dada, Futurist, Pop, Fred, Fabulous Five, Art, and Tomato.

Despite all the fanfare for graffiti writers, only a handful stand a chance of establishing themselves as artists. Among them, Futura 2000 is a prime contender.

As on only child, Futura, now 24, was adopted and raised by a white father and black mother on the upper West Side. "I was always a class clown," he says. "I always wanted to be the center of attention." Tonight, he is sitting in a bar near his old neighborhood wearing his usual uniform: baggy Army pants, basketball shoes, Lacoste shirt, and camouflage cap. "It's funny," he says taking a sip of beer, "but this is the same bar my father used to come to every night. He was an alcoholic."

After graduating from trade school at 16, Futura became a full-time graffiti artist. "I wasn't into drugs or crime," he says evenly, "but I always had a mischievous streak. I liked to run around construction sites when I was a kid. Writing had a daredevil quality I liked."

Break by Futura 2000, spraypaint on subway train, 1980, collection of Steven Hager.

In 1973, Futura and his best friend Ali were involved in a serious accident while painting a subway car in the early hours of the morning. A train suddenly started up and began moving, and the sparks ignited a hissing can of paint near Ali, who was instantly covered in flames. Futura helped his friend to the hospital, but Ali must have been in shock, because he told a *New York Times* reporter the next morning that he had learned his lesson and would never write graffiti again. Always a great story-teller, Ali also told the reporter that his sidekick had abandoned him to die in flames in the tunnel, which wasn't actually true, but it made the whole story much more dramatic if Ali had to save himself. Within a week, Futura had to join the navy and get out of town because nobody believed his side and there were many on the street who wanted to stomp him on sight. That was seven years ago.

Futura photographed by Stephen Crichlow in 1983.

Then, last year, Futura returned to New York and started writing again (at the suggestion of Ali, who felt the movement was gaining momentum again). *The Village Voice* ran a piece praising Futura's work, and CBS asked him to appear in a graffiti documentary that aired recently.

Futura finishes his beer and heads for a storefront near Columbus Avenue and 106th Street, to attend the weekly meeting of the Soul Artists, a club of writers spearheading the graffiti revival. Several writers have brought along their "piece books," which contain photographs of finished trains and sketches of new ideas; by the time Futura arrives, groups of four and five writers are gathered around each book, jockeying for position as the pages are turned. A radio is blasting in one corner and several bottles of wine are making the rounds. As is customary at these meetings, an odd assortment of outsiders has gathered. The writers are wary of them—especially when they're from the press. Asked his age, the writer Dondi informs a reporter, "That's not important. Only my work is important."

Ali appeared in a promotional fashion spread in New York magazine.

Ali—founder, leader and spokesman for Soul Artists—calls the meeting to order and introduces the main topic for discussion: How to stop the MTA from destroying the writers' murals. "How can the city spend $6 million a year removing our art when the subway don't even run on time?!" an angry Ali asks rhetorically. "They should take the money and put it into a preventative maintenance program." Ali and the other Soul Artists are lobbying for the legalization of subway graffiti. "We intend to submit a proposal to the MTA when our exhibit opens," he says.

The MTA, of course, remains singularly unimpressed with the artistic aspirations of the new breed of writers, and it is unlikely that Richard Ravitch will be on hand at the Mudd Club opening next week. Says Alfred Oliveri, head of the Transit Association's vandal squad: "The media has glorified these kids to the point where we are getting more and more of them. The trains are saturated with garbage. If this is art—then to hell with art!"

In fact, it seems that the more attention the graffiti writers get, the more determined the MTA is to thwart them. But the writers are unlikely to turn in their spray cans anytime soon. "I the early days, we never went down to the yards thinking we were artists," says Futura. "Now, everyone takes his work seriously."

Looking for the Perfect Beat

WE HEAR THE SOUNDS OF AN AUDIENCE MURMURING in anticipation of the start of something big.

> KOOL HERC (O.S.)
> *Test, test. It's the serious, serio-so joint-ski.*
> *You're listening to the sound system.*
> *(an echo chamber is turned on)*
> *The Hercoloids...loids...loids...*
> *And I just want to say to all my b-boys...oys...oys...*
> *Rock on.*

WE HEAR A LOUD HIP HOP BREAK. The music builds in intensity as it continues throughout the sequence.
FADE IN:
A HELICOPTER VIEW OF UPPER MANHATTAN ROOFTOPS, ala the opening of West Side Story. WE SEE THE EAST RIVER BELOW, and the urban landscape shifts from roofs to freeways and the bombed-out vacant lots around them.
EXT. SOUTH BRONX
"SOUTH BRONX 1980"
KENNIE SHAKLEFORD, RAMON FRANCO and CHOLLY WILSON walk down a side street on a clear, crisp day. They move with cocky, aggressive bravado -- like the style lords of the street that they are. A CLOSE SHOT ON Kennie, who is the leader of this three-man crew. He is 17 and black. Ramon, 16, is short and wears a hat tilted at a jaunty angle. He is Puerto Rican. Cholly, 17, wears sunglasses and is well-built. He is black. A WIDER ANGLE shows the neighborhood, which resembles a war zone. Rubble-strewn empty lots and burned-out buildings line the block. They cut through a vacant lot, climb a mound of rubble and walk down an alley. Cholly falls several steps behind. Kennie puts his arm around Ramon while talking to him. Cholly catches up and jumps between them, wrapping his arms around Kennie and Ramon. Ramon stops in front of a wall heavily marked with graffiti. He points at the names on the wall. Ramon removes a giant magic marker from his coat and signs: "DJ RAMO" on the wall. The signature is executed with considerable style. Cholly asks for the marker by Ramon refuses to give it to him. Cholly demands the marker. Ramon smiles and puts the marker in his pocket. Kennie grabs Ramon from behind while Cholly retrieves the marker. Cholly signs: "CHOLLY 167." Cholly's signature is a bit crude next to Ramon's. Cholly hands the marker to

Kennie, who signs "SOULSKI TOO." Kennie hands the marker back to Ramon.
A VARIETY OF ANGLES show the three walking down the street.
They enter a run-down, two-story house that is surrounded by larger buildings. The house has a small, dilapidated porch.
END OF SONG
INT. LIVINGROOM, THEODORE'S HOUSE
FROSTY and MEL, two black teenagers, are unraveling an electronic cable. They are standing in a large, empty room that has a dirty linoleum floor and no furniture. Sunlight streams through the bare window. The window panes are streaked with dirt. Two giant speakers for a customized sound system are stacked against one wall. Frosty and Mel set up two microphone stands.
INT. HALLWAY THEADORE'S HOUSE
Kennie, Ramon and Cholly enter the front door, walk down the hall and turn into the room.
INT. LIVINGROOM, THEODORE'S HOUSE
Kennie sees Frosty and Mel and stops abruptly. He looks perplexed. Kennie looks at Ramon, who shrugs his shoulders.

>   KENNIE
>   *Yo. Whatcha doin wit that mike?*

Mel looks at Frosty with a worried expression. Frosty unravels the mike cable and shows no emotion. He ignores Kennie.

>   KENNIE
>   *Where's Theodore?*
>   FROSTY
>   *In the back.*
>   KENNIE
>   (to Cholly)
>   *Stay here and keep and eye on this.*

Kennie and Ramon walk through an archway into an empty room that once served as a dining area. THEODORE and LEP are seated on milk crates that are filled with records. They are just finishing a marijuana cigarette laced with angel dust. Lep greets Kennie effusively. Although medicated, Theodore appears worried. He offers the joint to Kennie, but it's too small to even mess with.

>   KENNIE
>   *I smell mint. Is that dusted? You know*
>   *I don't be messin with no dust, bro,*
>   *why you dissin' me like dat?*
>   *Little Lep! My man! How you been?*
>   (they shake hands)

You know Ramon, my deejay.
                LEP
Sure, we met. I seen your tags. I like your style.
              KENNIE
           (to Ramon)
This is the baddest breaker I know. He got moves, man. Killer moves. His older brother was in the Zulu Kings with my brother.
(Lep nods his head sheepishly)
So how you been? How's the crew?
                LEP
They're okay. We're gonna battle Rockwell at the Heavalo. You gonna be there?
              KENNIE
You know it. Wassup with Theodore? How come he ain't said nothin? You too dusted to talk?
            THEODORE
Hi, Kennie. Wassup, Ramon?
An uncomfortable silence fills the room.
              KENNIE
Wassup with these boys out there, messin' with our mics?
            THEODORE
            (coughs)
Those be my new emcees.
              KENNIE
Now how can that be? When Cholly and me, we your emcees.
            THEODORE
Not no more. I just got these two yesterday. They got a record out and everthin'. And they was lookin for a deejay wit a system. They gonna let me be the deejay.

Lep stares at the ground. Kennie looks at Ramon. Ramon, who has been trying to get a hit off the minature joint suddenly swallows the roach, makes a stricken face, and then coughs it out.
              RAMON
Damn.

KENNIE
So what about the hookie party tomorrow?
THEODORE
They gonna be there. You wanna come, you can come. I'll put you down. You can do a show if you want, but you ain't gonna get down wit no money. Cause I got professional emcees now. And they gotta get the money.
KENNIE
Tell me. You heard they record? Whatta you think, Lep?
LEP
(shakes his head)
This between you two. I ain't involved.
KENNIE
(loud enough to hear in the next room)
I heard it. It's wack! It's NOT gettin over.
(to Theodore)
Anyway, I thought we had an agreement. Ramon here, he TAUGHT you how to deejay.
THEODORE
All I know is, you been talkin for months bout how we gonna play the Heavalo and you ain't played there yet. These guys done already played the Heavalo. Twice! They down with Herc. Times have changed. You gotta have a record to get over these days. And you ain't got no record.
KENNIE
Well, if that's how you feel...what can I say? It's your system ain't it?
THEODORE
It ain't nothin personal. You know

>   *I like you. But I gotta do what's*
>   *best for business.*
>   KENNIE
>   (pointing at tape cassette)
>   *That's my tape, right?*
>   THEODORE
>   *Take it.*
>   Kennie picks up the cassette.
>   KENNIE
>   (to Ramon)
>   *Let's go.*
>   (they exit)

INT. LIVINGROOM THEADORE'S HOUSE
Kennie and Ramon walk through the room, pointedly ignoring Frosty and Mel.
>   KENNIE
>   (to Cholly)
>   *Let's break out.*

EXT. STREET BY THEADORE'S
Kennie, Ramon and Cholly exit from the house. Kennie is animatedly explaining to Cholly that they have just lost their access to a sound system, which means they can't throw jams for their friends in the park anymore.

>   CHOLLY
>   *That sucker. I'm gonna crush him.*
>   KENNIE
>   *How we 'sposed to get a rep with no*
>   *sound system? He's turning into a*
>   *dust junkie anyway. We lucky to get*
>   *rid of him. You'll see.*

DISSOLVE TO:
INT. BEDROOM KENNIE'S HOUSE -- DAY
A CLOSE SHOT of a door. We hear a BANGING NOISE.

>   HELENE (O.S.)
>   *Kennie! Get up! I'm not gonna call*
>   *you again!*
>   KENNIE
>   *I'm up.*

ANGLE ON THE BED where Kennie has a blanket pulled over his head. He is not up. In fact, he is in danger of falling back asleep.
INT. HALLWAY KENNIE'S HOUSE
Kennie's mother, HELENE, walks away from the door while wiping her hands on a dishrag. She is a stout woman with a warm, trusting face. LEE SHAKLEFORD, 12, runs down the hallway. He is a bit hyperactive.

>
LEE
I'll get him.
HELENE
You get back to the table and
finish your breakfast.
Helene ushers Lee down the hallway.

INT. KENNIE'S BEDROOM -- DAY
The body underneath the blanket rolls over and moans. A WIDER ANGLE shows the interior of the room. It has two beds, two dressers and piles of junked electronic equipment, salvaged from the garbage. Kennie has converted some of this junk into a workable stereo. The walls of the room are plastered with flyers for rap shows. The names "Kool Herc" "Afrika Bambaataa" and "Grandmster Flash" appear prominently on the flyers.

INT. KENNIE'S KITCHEN

>
LEE
(playing with his cereal)
...and Danny said we didn't have to
go to school.
HELENE
(drying a glass)
What happened to Danny? He used to
be smart. Sounds like he's gonna
turn out like his brother.
LEE
I want to be a rapper like Kennie.
HELENE
(sighs)
What do you want to fool with that
silliness for? Your brother is
getting too old for it and you're
too young. I never heard anything

so ridiculous. It's just a fad.
It'll never take the place of real
singing.

Kennie enters the kitchen and throws his arms back in a monumental yawn. He reaches for a glass and fills it with water.

KENNIE
Don't you two ever get tired of
talkin bout me?

HELENE
Did you get your beauty sleep, Mr.
Brando?

LEE
Tell mom we don't have to go to
school.

KENNIE
Says who?

HELENE
Danny Wood.

KENNIE
Danny "wack attack" Wood. The
serious serio-so chumpski.

We hear a WHISTLE FROM THE STREET.

CUT TO:

EXT. STREET BY KENNIE'S
Ramon is whistling with his fingers in his mouth.

INT. KENNIE'S KITCHEN

KENNIE
Gotta go.
(kissing Helene)
Have a good day. Don't work too
hard.

EXT. STREET BY KENNIE'S
Ramon is waiting for Kennie to come out of his building. A small boy carrying a stick chases another boy across the street.

RAMON
(laughing)
Run Frankie! He's gaining on you!

Kennie emerges from his building. He greets Ramon and they walk down the street to the busstop.

KENNIE

> *Any luck locating a system?*
>
> RAMON
>
> *Naw.*
>
> KENNIE
>
> *Man, you better get on the case. Otherwise we might just have to find a new deejay. We sure could use one that knows how to cut.*
>
> RAMON
>
> *Who can cut wit emcees that can't keep the beat.*
>
> KENNIE
>
> *Who dat?*
>
> RAMON
>
> *You, bro.*

Kennie tries to knock Ramon's hat off, but Ramon deftly jumps out of reach and laughs.

EXT. ROOSEVELT HIGH SCHOOL

Students are pouring into the entrance of Roosevelt High. Located on Fordham Road, the school has a somewhat wild reputation. Most of the students are lower class blacks and Hispanics. Since a lot of drugs are sold nearby, security is strict inside the school. In fact, the atmosphere is closer to a reformatory than a high school. A bus stops in front of the school and ejects a crowd of kids carrying books. Kennie and Ramon are in the center of the group. They mount the steps to Roosevelt.

> KENNIE
>
> (looking ahead)
>
> *Just don't bump into anybody. We got Zulus on one side and Five Percenters on the other.*
>
> RAMON
>
> *How can you tell the Five Percenters?*
>
> KENNIE
>
> *They the ones always talkin' bout pork.*

INT. MATH CLASS

Kennie sits in the back of the class and doodles graffiti in a notebook. He stares out the window. A white subway train crosses the horizon in the distance.

INT. LUNCHROOM
A long line stretches down the hall into the lunchroom. No roughhousing is allowed during lunch period and a group of beefy gym teachers are standing by to insure order. The tables closest to the windows have been taken over by the football and basketball teams, who do not encourage uninvited visitors to sit with them. For the most part, girls and boys are at different tables, as are blacks, whites and Hispanics.
Kennie, Ramon and Cholly collect their lunch and find seats at the table reserved for the b-boys, the only fully integrated table in the room.

                    CHOLLY
       ...this guy was givin somethin out
           and I said, "I don't want that
             shit." This teacher hears me and
             right away takes the offensive. He
              wants to see my hall pass...
                     RAMON
        That's when he really started cursing.
                    CHOLLY
             No way. I did NOT curse.
                    KENNIE
                What did you say?
                    CHOLLY
            (carefully picking his words)
         I said: I'm not talkin to you and you
       better get out of my face or I will chair you.
Kennie and Ramon laugh. Kennie checks for the nearest gym teacher to make sure they aren't being overheard.
                    KENNIE
     That sounds like a minimum of a one day suspension to me.
                    CHOLLY
          If I DO get suspended, you better
                stay out wit me, bro.
                     RAMON
          Yo, we could hit the tunnels! You know
         the Transit Authority just started a new front
         on the graffiti wars. They painting cars they run
        through the buff all white. It's like the perfect backdrop,
           man. It's like they're handing us a fresh canvas
                      or somethin'.
                    CHOLLY
                 (slapping five)

179

*The search for a white train bomb, I'm down,
bro. But it should be a ten car masterpiece that flows
together as one giant, moving billboard. And that
means massive amounts of paint. And that means
rackin' up.*
                    KENNIE
*Before you risk your life and limb and a month
in Rikers, especially since the white cars are the most
heavily defended. Let us entertain an alternative
mission that doesn't involve potential jail time. I
suggest making the rounds at these local record
companies that are jumpin' on rap. And let if be known
this info comes direct from from Afrika Bambaataa hisself.*
Kennie pulls a piece of paper out of his pants pocket and
              shows it to Ramon and Cholly.
                    RAMON
           All right! I'm down wit this.

INT. RECORD COMPANY OFFICE
Kennie, Cholly and Ramon enter. Kennie talks to a receptionist. He holds up a tape cassette. The receptionist looks at the tape and shakes her head.
EXT. RECORD STORE
Kennie, Ramon and Cholly enter the store.
INT. RECORD STORE
Kennie talks to a bearded man sitting behind a counter. Kennie holds up a tape. The engineer shakes his head.
INT. RECORD COMPANY OFFICE
Kennie, Cholly and Ramon are grouped around a desk with two independent record producers. They shake their heads.
EXT. SNEAKER SHOP -- DUSK
A CLOSE SHOT on the window of a sneaker store. A wide variety of tennis, basketball and running shoes are on display.

                    RAMON
    Look at the space boots. Fresh! I want some.
                    CHOLLY
           Those Nikes are fresh too.
A WIDER ANGLE shows Kennie, Ramon and Cholly standing in front of the
                     store.
                    RAMON
    I was here last week and this homey ax for

*a pair of Kareems. He put one on and says:
"Damn! This shoe is TIGHT. Can I try a size
ten?" So the clerk goes into the back and
zoooom...that boy was GONE! It took him
less than five seconds to get off the block.
I never saw anyone run so fuckin' fast.*
                    KENNIE
          Let's walk by the Heavalo.
                    RAMON
             What for? It's closed.
                    KENNIE
       *Come on, it's only like five blocks
                  from here.*
           (looks back for Cholly)
*Hey! Will you hurry up! Why we always
got to wait for you? I got a grandmother
        that walks faster than you do.*
                    CHOLLY
           Yo, man. What's the hurry?
                    RAMON
       He wants to check out the Heavalo.
Cholly peers over the top of a pair of imaginary sunglasses. (He is performing
an imitation of Kool Herc, the deejay who runs the Heavalo.)
                    CHOLLY
        *Rock the house, my mellow. It's the
                  serio-so jointski.*

A LONG SHOT shows the three friends laughing and joking as
they turn the corner and proceed down Jerome Avemue to the
Heavalo.
EXT. THE BASE HOUSE
Two Casanova's are standing on the stoop that leads to their base house, where
they sell cocaine to people, some of whom want to come in and freebase inside.
This operation is mostly for the local highrollers and is a step up from street
dealers. You can also get weed, dust and heroin from the Casanovas.

                    CASANOVA
          *Yo, Cholly! Come in and join the
                  party, hahaha.*
                    CHOLLY
         *Unfortunately, I ain't got no funds
                wit me right now.*

Kennie, Ramon and Cholly walk past the base house.

                         RAMON
                What's going on in there?
                         CHOLLY
           You don't know? That's the new Casanova
            base house. They used to be a division of the
            Black Spades. I know people that walked in there
            with thousands of dollars and left with nuthin' but a
             sore throat and a sexually transmitted disease.
                         RAMON
             You mean, they gettin it ON in there?
                         KENNIE
              If a girl is strung out and gettin high for
              days and days, she'll get to a state where
                she'll do ANYTHING for a hit.
                         RAMON
             I snorted coke before, but I never
                        done base.
                         CHOLLY
                It's the ultimate high. Just ax
                       Richard Pryor.
                         KENNIE
             Being onstage in the flow, that is
                     the ultimate high.

EXT. THE HEAVALO
ANOTHER ANGLE shows the nightclub, located in a sprawling, one-story structure. A colorful sign over the door reads: "HEAVALO." A placard next to the door reads: "Next Friday! The Ultimate Jam! NYC's #1 Record Rappers! The Treacherous Three! Put the boogie in your body! Doors open at 10! Come in peace!" Kennie, Ramon and Cholly read the placard. Kennie trys to peer into a blacked-out window. Ramon inspects a graffiti tag on the side of the building. Cholly puts his hand on the doorknob and finds it unlocked. He opens the door a crack and peers inside.
INT. THE HEAVALO
CHOLLY'S POV. The Heavalo has a medium-sized, wooden dance floor, a long bar and a small stage, where the deejay sets up his equipment. The walls are glossy black with gold trim. A disco ball hangs from the ceiling. The room is empty.

                       KENNIE (O.S.)
                    Man, what you doin?

>   CHOLLY
>   *Yo, man, let's go in.*
>   KENNIE
>   *You must be crazy.*
>   CHOLLY
>   *Nobody's here.*

CUT TO:
INT. HEAVALO OFFICE
KOOL HERC, a large muscular black, is seated behind a desk. The walls are covered with autographed pictures of rap and disco celebrities. Herc is listening to the radio and opening his mail. He hums along with the record. He hears something, stops for a moment and listens. He turns down the radio and hears voices and footsteps on the stage.
INT. THE HEAVALO
Kennie is standing on the stage holding an empty mike stand in one hand. Ramon stomps his feet, slaps his hands and lays down a beat with a human beatbox routine. Kennie and Cholly launch into their favorite rap routine.

>   KENNIE
>   *Yo check it out. We rockin the Heavalo.*
>   (he raps between his beat-box sounds)
>   *We throw down hard and I aim to
>   please,*
>   CHOLLY
>   *with finesse, to impress, the young
>   la-dies.*
>   KENNIE
>   *We got rhymes galore and much, much
>   more. So eliminate the possibility,*
>   CHOLLY
>   *...there exists emcees wit more
>   consistency...*

The door to the office opens. Kool Herc peers out. He looks over the top of his sunglasses in the same manner imitated by Cholly. A CLOSE SHOT of Kennie as he starts to ham up his rap routine. Kennie's eyes are closed. He is pretending it is Friday night and he is onstage at the Heavalo.

>   KENNIE
>   *Put you hands in the air and listen to me,
>   cause you're listening to the sounds of the*

> mighty Soulski. I want you to get loose,
> get ready to rock. I'm gonna paralyze
> your mind and put you in shock.
>   KOOL HERC
> The club is closed guys, okay?

Kennie's performance grinds to a halt as he realizes he is being watched. He sheepishly moves the mike stand to the rear of the stage. Ramon and Cholly have backed up all the way to the door.

EXT. STREET BY HEAVALO

A LONG SHOT shows Kennie, Cholly and Ramon leaving the Heavalo. Cholly does an imitation of Kool Herc peering over the top of his glasses. Ramon imitates Kennie rapping on the mike and doing a double-take on Kool Herc. Cholly says goodbye and splits off. Kennie and Ramon continue to the busstop.

EXT. BUSSTOP

Kennie and Ramon wait for the bus. Ramon gets out his school bus pass. ANOTHER ANGLE shows the arrival of SMITTY AND THE CASANOVAS. Smitty is a bit bored and looking for someone to pick on. Kennie senses this and tenses as Smitty walks by. Smitty looks at Kennie but says nothing. After Smitty passes, Kennie shows signs of relief. Suddenly, however, Smitty turns and walks back to Ramon. He stares at the bus pass in Ramon's hand.

> SMITTY
> *Yo, man. What's that in your hand?*
> *A bus pass. Can I take a look at that?*
> Ramon doesn't know what to say. He looks to Kennie for help.
> KENNIE
> (mildly, to Smitty)
> *Wassup?*
> SMITTY
> *What you mean, wassup?*
> KENNIE
> *Nuthin'. This is my homie...*
> SMITTY
> *Why don't choo mind your own bizness?*
> *Did I ax YOU wassup? What if I was to*
> *punch you in the mowf, right now?*
> KENNIE
> *Yo, yo, peace.*
> CASANOVA !
> *Deck him.*

CASANOVA 2
Yo, punch him.
RAMON
(hands over the pass)
This what you want?
SMITTY
For me? Thank you. I could use this even though I'm not in school no more, hahaha.
(to Kennie)
Don't fuck with the Casanovas.
Smitty feints a punch at Kennie's mouth, causing Kennie to recoil slightly. The Casanovas laugh hysterically.
CASANOVA 1
Shit, bro! He just disrespected you big time! What are you, soft? Don't take that shit!
The Casanovas urge Kennie to defend his honor but Kennie ignores them.
CASANOVA 3
Let 'em slide. I seen 'em throwing jams in Echo Park.
The gang walks off. One looks back at Kennie and snickers.
KENNIE
You coulda avoided that.
RAMON
What did I do?
KENNIE
(pissed)
Why'd you take that pass out anyway? Didn't you see 'em comin? Stupid!
They wait for the bus in silence.

INT. KENNIE'S BEDROOM -- NIGHT

A CLOSE SHOT of Kennie's back. He is half buried in his closet and trying to retrieve a box he has carefully hidden.
LEE (O.S.)
What you lookin for?
KENNIE
Nuthin' that would interest you.
Kennie yanks hard on a box that has other boxes stacked on top of it. It finally breaks free. Kennie prys open the top, revealing several cans of spray paint.
LEE
I know what you been doin'. Graffiti

    taggin'. Mom'll kill you if she finds out.
Kenny selects two cans and puts the box back in the closet.
        KENNIE
   But mom will not find out. And if she does,
   I'll know just who to give a beat-down to.
        LEE
   Are you goin to the Heavalo tomorrow?
        KENNIE
       Maybe.
        LEE
   Maybe I won't tell mom if you take
      me wit you.
        KENNIE
   You're too young. They wouldn't let
      you in the door.

We hear a WHISTLE FROM THE STREET. Kennie pokes his head out the window.
CUT TO:
EXT. STREET BY KENNIE'S -- NIGHT
KENNIE'S POV. Ramon is standing outside the window.

        KENNIE
      (loud whisper)
     Where's Cholly?
        RAMON
   He's gonna meet us on the platform.

CUT TO:
INT. KENNIE'S BEDROOM -- NIGHT
Kennie puts the paint into a messenger bag.
INT. HALLWAY KENNIE'S HOUSE
Kennie bounds down the stairs.
EXT. STREET BY KENNIE'S -- NIGHT
Kennie comes running out of the building. Ramon is waiting impatiently. They jog down the center of the street. The SOUNDTRACK SWELLS and contines through the next few subway sequences.
CUT TO:
EXT. ELEVATED TRAIN TRACKS -- NIGHT
A subway train roars past. It gleams in the moonlight. The sides of the train are splattered with graffiti. Kennie and Ramon are sitting on a bench waiting for a train.

Ramon has his tag book on his lap and his showing Kennie his plan for a 10-car masterpiece called: The History of Hip Hop.
The first three cars are tributes to Kool Herc, Afrika Bambaataa and Grandmaster Flash. The next three are tributes to graffiti, breakdancing and rap music. DJ Ramo, Soulski and Cholly 167 appear prominently on the final car.

> KENNIE
> *Damn that's nice. You really worked on this one.*
> *And I like the way you used different writers styles*
> *for different cars.*
> RAMON
> *Yeah, like you see Taki and Stay High*
> *on the Kool Herc car, but when you get*
> *to Flash's car, it's Dondi, Blade and Zephyr.*
> *Can you imagine when this is up and running?*
> *It would give us a rep all over the city overnight.*
> *This is how you make it, bro. You make a*
> *statement that can't be ignored.*

INT. SUBWAY CAR
Cholly stands alone in the empty train. He is carrying a ghetto blaster. Cholly looks out the window. CHOLLY'S POV. The battle-scarred landscape of the South Bronx flashes by. TRAIN'S POV. A MOVING SHOT taken from the front of the train. The projects and tenements of the Bronx are silhouetted against a dark blue sky. The tracks rapidly disappear underneath the train, creating an illusion of even greater speed than the train is actually traveling. ANOTHER ANGLE shows Kennie and Ramon waiting on the platform for the train to arrive. ANGLE ON TRAIN as it turns a wide corner and slows down. The train screeches to a halt. The doors fly open. Kennie and Ramon board the front car and greet Cholly. A window opens. The conductor appears and checks to see that the doors are clear. The doors close. CLOSE SHOT on the wheels of the train as it starts to pull out of the station. Kennie, Ramon and Cholly are top-rocking against each other inside the car. TRAIN'S POV as it dives into a dark tunnel at 149th Street. The pillars of the tunnel flash by, illuminated by the train's headlights.
INT. 42ND STREET SUBWAY STATION
The train screeches to a halt. Kennie, Cholly and Ramon get off.
EXT. 42ND STREET -- NIGHT
Kennie and Ramon walk past an array of hustlers, drug pushers, pickpockets, junkies, prostitutes. Cholly follows several steps behind. They stop in front of a street performer who is doing an imitation of Stevie Wonder. A policeman handcuffs a belligerent drunk.

                    DRUNK
        My car's right there, officer. Just let me
        drive around until I can sober up a bit.

INT. SUBWAY CAR
Kennie, Cholly and Ramon are standing in a crowded subway car. A tall black man wearing a knitted skull cap and white robes is soliciting for a Muslim daycare center. No one offers him anything. Kennie takes some change out of his pocket and gives it to him.
EXT. WASHINGTON SQUARE PARK
The park is filled with a weird combination of street people, preppies, beatniks, freaks and b-boys. Kennie, Ramon and Cholly wander through the crowd, passing a folk singer and a group of pot dealers. KENNIE'S POV. A large crowd stands around the circular fountain at the center of the park. The fountain is empty of water and being used as a dance floor. Kennie walks closer to investigate. We hear A DISCO SONG BEING PLAYED ON A GHETTO BLASTER. Kennie nudges his way to the front row. TRACY and her friend LISA are dancing. Tracy is a tall black girl with a model's face. She is obviously a well-trained jazz dancer. Although she is dancing for fun, not money, some people throw coins into the fountain.
ANGLE ON KENNIE, who can't take his eyes off Tracy.
ANGLE ON A DERELICT, who dances into the fountain. He dances over to the coins, leans over and picks them up. The crowd laughs. Tracy smiles.

                    CHOLLY
                (finding Kennie)
        There you are. Ramon wants to
                    split.
                (pause, no response)
            Come on. This is wack.
                    KENNIE
        Yo, check it out. That girl can
                really dance.
ANGLE ON TRACY AND LISA talking.
                    CHOLLY
                She's okay.
Kennie and Tracy establish eye contact. Suddenly, a tall handsome white boy enters the scene, puts his arm around Tracy. They obviously know each other well.
                    CHOLLY

>   *You're out of luck, homey.*
>   KENNIE
>   *What?*
>   CHOLLY
>   *The white boy got her.*
>   KENNIE
>   *What choo talkin bout? You think I*
>   *want her?*
>   RAMON
>   (suddenly appearing)
>   *Yo, let's break out. I want to hit*
>   *the layup.*

ANGLE ON TRACY. Although the boy is talking to her, Tracy doesn't seem to be paying complete attention. She looks back at the spot where she saw Kennie. TRACY'S POV on an empty spot in the crowd just vacated by Kennie.
INT. SUBWAY STATION
SOUNDTRACK SWELLS as Kennie, Ramon and Cholly jump the turnstiles without paying. The token clerk sees them.
TOKEN CLERK
Hey, get back here you punks!
Kennie, Cholly and Ramon sprint down the stairs, barreling though a group of people moving in the opposite direction. ANOTHER ANGLE shows a train parked in the station with its doors open. Kennie jumps into the train just as the doors are closing. He holds the door open long enough for Cholly and Ramon to squeeze inside. VARIOUS SHOTS of the train moving uptown. The train stops at 96th and Broadway. Kennie, Cholly and Ramon walk to the end of the platform on the downtown side of the tracks. Kennie is about to jump onto the tracks when Ramon grabs his arm.

>   RAMON
>   *Careful.*
>   (points across platform)

KENNIE'S POV. A transit cop walks the platform on the uptown side. They wait for the cop to leave by pretending to be waiting for a train. THE MUSIC SWELLS. As soon as the coast is clear, Kennie, Ramon and Cholly leap on the tracks and start running down the tunnel. They have to race to an abandoned station before another downtown train comes through.
INT. SUBWAY TUNNEL
Kennie leads the way down the dark tunnel in a race against death. He has to be careful not to stumble and touch the third rail, which pulses with over 700 volts

of electricity. An uptown train, running on the track next to them, roars past going the other direction. The headlights of the train flash through the pillars, creating a strobe effect on Kennie's face, which radiates with exhilaration.
INT. ABANDONED STATION
After a brief sprint, they arrive at a station that is no longer in service. (The street entrance was sealed over ten years ago, and the only entrance to this station is through the tunnel.) The station has become a favorite spot for graffiti writers to leave their tags. Kennie and Cholly scramble up the concrete wall onto the platform. Ramon produces a can of paint and starts spraying: "DJ RAMO." Kennie sprays "SOULSKI TOO." ANOTHER ANGLE. Ramon is standing on the train tracks. He is using a magic marker to write his tag on all the steel pillars in the station. ANGLE ON CHOLLY, who is exploring some old graffiti marks in a corner of the station.

                CHOLLY
            Check this out!
Kennie comes over to investigate.
KENNIE'S POV. A series of old, faded graffiti tags, including "SUPER KOOL" and "STAY HIGH 149."
                CHOLLY
    These tags are really old. Look at that
    Stay High. That's one writer I always wanted
    to meet. Whata ya think happened to him?
                KENNIE
    He works at the World Trade Center.
      His real name is Wayne.
                CHOLLY
    Yeah, what's he do at the Trade Center?
                KENNIE
    I'm not sure. I think he's a messenger
    or sumthin'. Hey, where's Ramon?

CUT TO:
INT. SUBWAY TUNNEL
A subway train is roaring towards the abandoned station.
CUT TO:
Ramon writing on the pillars, oblivious to the approaching danger.
KENNIE'S POV. The train barrels into the station. It does not stop or slow down. Kennie looks at the other end of the station and sees Ramon in the distance, still standing on the tracks.

                        KENNIE
                  LOOK OUT RAMON!

KENNIE'S POV. From this angle it's impossible to tell what happened to
Ramon, although it seems likely he was struck by the train. Kennie has to wait
for all ten cars to pass before he can find out. Eventually, Ramon emerges back
onto the tracks from between two pillars he was hiding behind. He smiles and
waves.

                        KENNIE
              Damn! You scared the shit out of me!

INT. 96TH STREET SUBWAY STATION
Kennie, Ramon and Cholly come running out of the tunnel and leap onto the
platform. ANOTHER ANGLE shows the arrival of a train headed uptown to
the Bronx. Kennie, Ramon and Cholly get on.
INT. SUBWAY TRAIN
The train is crowded. Kennie, Cholly and Ramon stand in the corner.
RAMON'S POV. Three pretty PUERTO RICAN GIRLS area sitting in the
center of the car. Ramon nudges Kennie and points at the girls discreetly.
Kennie and Cholly look at the girls. Ramon struts through the car and stops in
front of the girls. He smiles at the prettiest one. She ignores him.

                        RAMON
                         Hi.
                     (no response)
                You girls headed uptown?
                     (no response)
              I happen to be traveling with one of
              the most famous rappers in the Bronx.
            You like rap music? Ever heard of Soulski?
                        GIRL 1
                        Who?
                        RAMON
               That's him standing right there...

GIRL'S POV. Kennie and Cholly smile. Cholly waves. Kennie wonders what

Ramon is saying to them.

> RAMON
> *...and he ax me to introduce you to him.
> See, I think he has a crush on you.*
> GIRL 2
> *Why don't you find somebody else to
> bother?*
> GIRL 1
> (all smiles)
> *Maybe we should introduce him to
> our friends?*

The train pulls to a stop at 125th Street. The girls get out. Ramon motions to his friends to exit. Kennie is reluctant at first, but gets off the train.

INT. 125TH STREET SUBWAY STATION

The girls whisper to each other as they climb the stairs out of the station. Kennie, Ramon and Cholly follow.

> RAMON
> (frantic whisper)
> *I call dibs on the one on the right.*
> KENNIE
> *What did she say to you anyway? Are
> we supposed to be followin' them?*
> RAMON
> *She said she had some friends she
> wanted us to meet.*

EXT. 125TH STREET
The girls emerge from the subway and walk down the street. One of the girls turns around to make sure that Ramon and his friends are still following.
EXT. SCHOOL BASKETBALL COURT
The girls turn into the playground. At the back of the playground are ten members of the SAVAGE SKULLS, a local street gang. They are wearing Levi jackets with gang insignias on the back and drinking quarts of Old English malt liquor. The girls approach the gang and start talking and pointing back at Ramon and his friends.
ANGLE ON RAMON, stopping in his tracks. RAMON'S POV. Girl 2 is talking to the LEADER of the gang. She points a Ramon. The leader starts putting on leather gloves. ANGLE ON RAMON, who spins around 360 degrees with a look of sudden panic.

                                    RAMON
                    Wait 'till we get to the gate. Then run
                    like the fuckin' wind back to the subway
                station. If we get split up we meet at Kennie's.
                                    KENNIE
                        Why you always gettin' me into this
                                      shit?
                                    CHOLLY
                        Look around for a pipe or stick or
                        somthin in case they catch you.
                                    KENNIE
                              Nobody's catchin me.
ANGLE ON THE GANG, as they methodically merge, whisper to each other.
Kennie, Ramon and Cholly reach the gate and break out running. The gang
takes off after them. Kennie, Ramon and Cholly sprint towards the subway
entrance, while the gang follows close on their heels. ANGLE ON the three
                            girls, who are amused.
                                    GIRL 2
                                Run suckas.
ANGLE ON THE GANG stopping momentarily at the subway entrance. A few
enter the same subway station as the three fugitives. The rest split up to cover
          the other nearby subway entrances to block any attempted escape.
                      INT. 125TH STREET SUBWAY STATION
                   Kennie, Ramon and Cholly jump the turnstile.
                                    RAMON
                               (to the Token Clerk)
                     Call the cops! The Skulls are after us!

ANGLE ON TOKEN CLERK, who looks confused. ANOTHER ANGLE
shows five Savage Skulls in hot pursuit. They hop the turnstile. ANGLE ON
THE CLERK, who looks dumbfounded and does nothing.
INT. 125TH STREET SUBWAY STATION
Kennie, Ramon and Cholly skid to a stop at the end of the platform. They look
up and see three Savage Skulls at the other end of the platform.

                                    RAMON
                        There's only one way out of here.
                                    KENNIE
                                 The tunnel.

They quietly slip onto the tracks without being seen and take off down the dark
tunnel. ANOTHER ANGLE shows the Savage Skulls walking up and down the

platform, hunting their prey. The various units meet up at the center of the platforms and are surprised at not finding the prey anywhere.

SKULLS LEADER
Where the fuck they go?

EXT. STREET BY KENNIE'S -- NIGHT
Ramon, Kennie and Cholly emerge from a subway entrance. They congratulate each other on a fine escape. They split up to go home.
KENNIE
See ya at 9 o'clock!

INT. PARK AVE LIVINGROOM
The livingroom of a lavishly furnished apartment on Park Avenue and 77th Street. A row of picture windows runs the length of the room. Helene wearily crosses the room wearing a coat and hat.
INT. PARK AVE DEN
MRS. FIELD, a haughty woman in her late 50's is seated at an antique desk. She is preparing a party list.

HELENE
*Excuse me, Mrs. Field. If that's
everything, I'll be leaving.*
MRS. FIELD
*Is it five already? Did you remember
to mend the shirt Mr. Field left on his dresser?*
HELENE
Yes ma'am.
MRS. FIELD
*You can go then. Oh. Helene. On Monday,
try and get here by eight. I'm having a dinner
on Sunday and they'll be lots of work for you.*
HELENE
Yes ma'am.
(she exits.)

Mrs. Field returns to her paperwork.
EXT. PARK AVENUE
Helene emerges from a high-rise apartment building. She is drained and exhausted. A limo pulls up to the curb. The doorman opens the door and tips his hat. Helene turns the corner and walks to the subway.
INT. SUBWAY STATION

Helene waits for the train.
INT. SUBWAY CAR
It is rush hour and Helene is unable to get a seat, even though several young men are seated near her. The train stops at 96th Street, where most of the white people get off, leaving some empty seats on the train so that Helene can sit down at last. THREE B-BOYS get on, one of whom is carrying a ghetto blaster. His machine is playing rap music at full volume. The b-boys stand in the doorway between cars. Helene gives them an angry look. HELENE'S POV. The b-boys are laughing, passing a joint and moving to the beat of the song. They start top-rocking while the train is moving.
EXT. STREET BY KENNIE'S -- NIGHT
Helene walks wearily up 167th Street, a sack of groceries on one arm. She passes some Hispanic men playing dominoes on a stoop.
INT. HALLWAY KENNIE'S HOUSE
Helene unlocks the door to her apartment. She opens the door and we hear the faint SOUND OF A RECORD BEING PLAYED.
INT. KENNIE'S KITCHEN
Helene drops the bag of groceries on the counter. She follows the sound of the music around the corner and down the hall. She stops outside her sons' room. Helene opens the door. THE MUSIC IS BLASTING. Kennie and Lee are top-rocking to "Just Begun" by Jimmy Castor.

LEE
(excited)
Mom! Look at this move!
(shows his footwork)
HELENE
Turn off the music!
The boys don't respond and keep dancing. Helene angrily crosses to the stereo and wrenches the needle off the record.
LEE
Aww, mom. Kennie was teaching me to top rock.
HELENE
(furious)
Lee, go in the kitchen and set the table.
LEE
Awww, can't we just do one more dance?

Helene grabs Lee by the arm and pulls him out of the room. Kennie is perplexed by his mother's behavior. He slowly puts the record away.

INT. KENNIE'S KITCHEN
Helene, Kennie and Lee are finishing dinner. Kennie and Lee are quiet because Helene is in a bad mood. Kennie wolfs down his dinner, takes his plate to the sink and washes the dish.

> HELENE
> *And why are you in such a rush?*
> KENNIE
> *I promised Ramon and Cholly I'd meet them in a hour. And I still got to shower. We're goin to the Heavalo tonight.*
> HELENE
> *You shouldn't be goin to that place.*
> KENNIE
> *Why not?*
> HELENE
> *I've heard the stories. I know what goes on there.*
> KENNIE
> *I don't know what you been hearin but it's a lot safer there than it is on the street around here.*

INT. KENNIE'S BATHROOM
Kennie is taking a shower and brushing his teeth at the same time.
INT. KENNIE'S BEDROOM -- NIGHT
Kennie, wearing only a pair of Lee jeans, is ironing his shirt.
A SERIES OF CUTS OF KENNIE GETTING DRESSED.
THE SNEAKERS
Kennie opens a package of new shoe laces and elaborately weaves the new laces into his basketball shoes. Kennie uses a toothbrush dipped in bleach to clean the edges of his sneakers until they look new.
THE CHAIN
Kennie places a gold chain around his neck. It reads: "SOULSKI."
THE SOCKS
Kennie pulls on two pair of white tube socks. (He needs two pair to lift the tongue on his sneakers to the proper height.)
THE HAT
Kennie carefully places a cap at the proper tilt.
THE BELT
Kennie threads a Garrison belt around his waist. It has a brass buckle with "SOULSKI" on it.

THE CONDOM slips into a back pocket.
INT. THE HEAVALO
We hear "WALKING ON SUNSHINE" BOOMING OUT OF A DISCO SOUND SYSTEM. The soundtrack is at peak volume. A CLOSE SHOT shows a white glove against a black background. The glove is moving in a weird, contorted manner. The glove is connected to a black wrist and arm. The arm pulses with energy. A WIDER ANGLE reveals an electric boogie dancer. The dancer moves effortlessly across the floor with the grace of a trained mime. The Heavalo has just opened but the dance floor is already packed. In two hours the club will be a sweatbox. The room is dark and filled with smoke. A number of local rap celebrities are already gathering on the deejay platform. Kool Herc stands at the center. All incoming males are frisked before being admitted to the club. The crowd is a tough, aggressive one. Many gangsters are known to frequent the Heavalo.
EXT. THE HEAVALO -- NIGHT
A long line is stretched around the block. Kennie, Ramon and Cholly are frisked as they enter. After paying their money, the three friends move straight to the deejay platform to see which rap celebrities are in attendance. Ramon tries to walk up the steps of the deejay platform but is repulsed by a bouncer. He trys to say hello to Herc, but is ignored. The b-boys are pressed around the stage. The older crowd, some of whom are dressed like pimps, stand at the bar. A man with a huge velvet hat is doing a line of coke on the bar. Everyone is acting super cool.

                    MAN AT BAR
Hey homey, wassup?
                        PIMP
Ain't nuthin' my brother, ain't nuthin.
ANGLE ON KOOL HERC as he steps to the microphone.
                    KOOL HERC
                (with echo chamber)
Yes, yes y'all. It's the serious, serioso jointski. You're listening to the sound system: The Hercoloids...oids..oids. And I just want to say to all my b-boys...oys...oys...Rock on. Time to get down to the AM. But please remember. Respect my system and I'll respect you and yours...and now as I scan the place, I see the

> *very familiar face of my mellow...ow...ow....Wallace Dee in the house. Wallace Dee, freak for me.*

Herc mixes into a James Brown record that is a favorite for top rocking. The crowd goes crazy and breaks out into a riot of top rocking. Kennie, Ramon and Cholly top rock against each other. A SERIES OF ANGLES SHOW THE DANCERS. The dance styles include the freak, electric boogie, top rocking and James Brown imitations.

One girl is in a freak sandwich between two boys. The three are close to having sexual relations since their bodies are pressed so close together. The men on the deejay platform clap their hands and urge the crowd to go crazy. A "scratch" deejay experiments with a record. A break dancer does several back flips and a circle forms
around him. ANGLE ON DEEJAY PLATFORM as the TREACHEROUS THREE approach the microphones. They launch into a rap routine. The crowd surges to the stage. The focus shifts from the b-boys to the rappers. A SERIES OF ANGLES show the group performing and the reactions of the crowd. KENNIE'S POV. Kennie watches the group from the front row. Kennie is overcome by a combination of envy and adulation. The performance ends. Kennie manuevers his way towards backstage. Ramon spots a pretty girl standing alone and moves toward her.

ENTER Smitty, who moves to speak with Cholly.

> SMITTY
> (slaps five)
> *Cholly, my mellow. Everythin everythin?*
> CHOLLY
> *You know it. Where's the crew?*
> SMITTY
> *They comin. Ain't you ready to get down wit the Casanovas yet? We're having a special private party at our crib after the show. Free blow, base and beer.*
> CHOLLY
> *Can I bring my crew, Soulski and Ramon?*
> SMITTY
> *Naww, not them. But you invited.*
> RAMON
> (to girl)

Hi.
(she ignores him)
Wanna dance?
(pause)
You come here often? I never seen you before.
(pause)
I guess you don't recognize me. I'm Deejay....
(she walks away)
Kennie has moved to the rear of the stage. He is standing near the Treacherous Three, eavesdropping on their conversation.

FAN
So when is your new record gonna come out?
KOOL MO DEE
Dunno. We got jerked on the last one. We just changed companies.
SPECIAL K
I heard Atomic records was lookin to sign a rapper but they don't want a crew, just one dude, like a new Kurtis Blow.
FAN
Who runs Atomic?
KOOL MO DEE
His name is Bither. Something Bither.
SPECIAL K
We wasn't businesswise before, but now we know what's happenin. It's all about the publishing. Seems like every hole-in-the-wall record company jumping on rap because of Rapper's Delight goin platinum an shit. You know they ripped off Caz, right? He ain't gettin a dime.
KOOL MO DEE
That's right.

Ramon approaches another girl, who walks away from him before he can deliver an opening line. Kool Herc plays APACHE and two break dance crews come out on the floor to do batte. A SERIES OF ANGLES on the break dancers competing against each other. The battle starts with everyone, but is soon narrowed down to the two best breakers from each crew going one on one against each other. One of them is Little Lep. Little Lep wins the battle with an amazing series of acrobatic moves.

EXT. STREET BY HEAVALO -- JUST BEFORE DAWN
The Heavalo is closing for the night. A crowd has collected on the street. Kennie Ramon and Cholly exit together. They pool enough change to go into the doughnut store that is just opening for business and get some freshly baked doughnuts. They argue over what flavors to buy. Kennie carries the bag out of the shop. Cholly and Ramon try and take it from him. They each grab a doughnut out of the bag and wolf it down.

INT. HALLWAY KENNIE'S HOUSE
Kennie, Ramon and Cholly race up the stairs to the roof.

EXT. KENNIE'S ROOF -- DAWN
Kennie, Cholly and Ramon sit on the edge of the building and look out over the South Bronx.

KENNIE'S POV. Many of the surrounding buildings are scarred by fire. Several nearby lots are empty and filled with rubble and trash. An elevated subway track is visible in the distance.

                KENNIE
*Don't it seem like we just turned around
one day and the whole damn neighborhood
was gone?*
                RAMON
The blackout. That's what got it all started.
                CHOLLY
*Are you serious? This has been happening
for as long as I been here. It's the fuckin
landlords, man. They be collectin some serious
insurance money.*
                KENNIE
*It's like someone with real feelings don't
even belong here no more.*

A freshly-painted white train appears on the elevated tracks in the distance. The train has been painted to cover graffiti marks.

                RAMON
*Man! A white one! Check it out! We gotta
go search for the layup that line feeds into.*
                CHOLLY
Yo, sun's comin up.

THE CAMERA PANS the jagged skyline as the sun's rays begin to light up the eastern sky.

INT. CASANOVA BASE HOUSE

There's a knock on the door. One of the Casanovas opens it a crack to see who is there, and then lets LONNIE in. THE CAMERA follows Lonnie as he walks through a trashed-out living room into the kitchen where Smitty is standing behind a counter selling coke and offering to cook it up for base. Lonnie puts forty dollars on the counter. Smitty pockets the money and starts cooking Lonnie's base on the stove.

EXT. ATOMIC RECORDS STOREFRONT -- DAY

Kennie enters the building carrying a ghetto blaster.

INT. ATOMIC RECORDS RECEPTION ROOM

Howie is seated at a desk. A girl is loading promotional records into a cardboard box. The walls are covered with record advertisements.

> HOWIE
> *Can I help you?*
> KENNIE
> *Yeah. I'd like to see a Mr. Bither?*
> HOWIE
> *Is he expecting you?*
> KENNIE
> *No. But I heard he lookin for a single rapper.*
> *I wanted...I wanted to play my tape for him.*
> HOWIE
> *Give it to me. I'll see that he gets it.*
> KENNIE
> *It's a rap song I wrote. I heard he was looking*
> *for a rapper. I'm Soulski.*
> HOWIE
> *Yeah, that's true about him looking for a rapper.*
> *Just write your name and phone number on the tape.*
> *Here's a pen.*
> KENNIE
> *This tape is guaranteed to go over*
> *in the Bronx. Believe me.*
> HOWIE
> *Yeah? If you're so good, how come I*
> *never heard of you, Soulski?*
> KENNIE
> *You will. You will. Just make sure*
> *Mister Bither lissens to this, okay?*

EXT. STREET BY ATOMIC RECORDS
Kennie exits with a happy smile. He's convinced his big break is coming soon. KENNIE'S POV on a girl in tights walking down the street. It's Tracy, the girl from the park. He crosses the street to intersept her. Kennie starts walking alongside her.

> TRACY
> *Excuse me. Do I know you? Are you following me?*
> KENNIE
> *I don't know. Where you headed?*
> TRACY
> *I don't think that's any of your business.*
> KENNIE
> *I saw you dancin in Washington Square Park yesterday. You're good. I know what I'm talkin bout. I'm a pretty good dancer myself.*

Tracy arrives at a doorway that leads up to a second floor dance studio. She stops.

> TRACY
> *Well, it certainly was interesting not meeting you.*

She starts up the stairs.

> KENNIE
> *Hey, wait a minute. Don't you want to give me your phone number?*

INT. DANCE STUDIO
A group of students are warming up in front of a mirrored wall. A dance instructor is talking to a young dancer. Enter Tracy. Kennie arrives a few seconds behind her.

> INSTRUCTOR
> (to Tracy)
> *Here's our star! Late, as usual. Please warm up quickly, dear. I want the class to see the new routine we've been working on. This is the number that's going to get you into the Dance Theater of Harlem, guaranteed.*

Several students notice Kennie with his ghetto blaster. They give him some strange looks. Kennie watches from the doorway while Tracy stretches on the bar.

> INSTRUCTOR
> *Who's your friend?*
> TRACY
> *Him? He's dancer. I think he wants to try out for the class?*
> INSTRUCTOR
> *Really? Somehow he doesn't look like an advanced student. Maybe he should try out for a beginner class instead.*
> TRACY
> *He says he is quite good.*

The instructor puts on a disco record.
VARIOUS ANGLES of Tracy demonstrating a part of her new routine. The instructor moves across the room and approaches Kennie.

> INSTRUCTOR
> *Try outs are on Thursdays.*
> TRACY
> *Oh, comeon. Let him try-out.*
> KENNIE
> (scoffs)
> *I can't dance to disco.*
> (looks disgusted)
> INSTRUCTOR
> *Oh yeah? Well, we have all varieties of music here. What sort are you looking for?*
> KENNIE
> *Have you got this?*

Kennie puts his ghetto blaster on the dance floor and turns it up full volume. WE HEAR THE B-BOY ANTHEM "JUST BEGUN" by Jimmy Castor. Kennie starts by top rocking. ANOTHER ANGLE on the students reacting. Kennie suddenly dives to the floor and begins doing backspins and hand spins. The class is amazed. Tracy smiles. The instruction applauds and shakes his head in disbelief. Kennie finishes with a freeze. The entire class applauds.
TIME LAPSE

                    INSTRUCTOR
            Any time you want to come back...
          I'm just so glad Tracy brought you by...
ANOTHER ANGLE on the class practicing break dance moves. Tracy is
                   packing up her gear to go.
                      STUDENT
            Kennie, can you show us that swipe
              one more time before you go?
                       KENNIE
          Actually, I got to bust out...But I'll be
                   back next week...

Kennie follows Tracy out the door.
EXT. STREET BY ATOMIC RECORDS
Kennie runs to catch up to Tracy.

                       KENNIE
         You really put me on the spot, didn't you?
                       TRACY
        Yeah, but it worked out okay though, didn't it?
                       KENNIE
          I'm actually a rapper now, by the way.
          I don't dance like I used to. You should
             have seen me when I was in my prime.
                       TRACY
                Really, when was that?
                       KENNIE
         About two years ago. We used to break on
           the concrete at Crotona Park. Our shirts
           would get all tore up and we'd have cuts
         on our arms and shoulders from all the bits of
             broken glass. We called em battle scars.
            Now it seems stupid to tear up your clothes
              just because you hear "Apache" come on.
             Now I leave that for the middle school
          crowd. Hey, how would you like to check out
              the Heavalo on Friday night wit me?
                       TRACY
                    What's that?

                    KENNIE
       Damn. Where you been girl? Never heard
        of the hottest club in the Bronx, where the
         godfather hisself, Kool Herc presides over
                the wheels of steel?
                     TRACY
       Actually, I don't think I've ever BEEN to
                    the Bronx.
                    KENNIE
        By Friday, I'll probably be celebrating
         my first record deal. I just dropped my
             tape off at Atomic Records.
                     TRACY
         And now you're gonna tell me you
             sing as well as you dance?
                    KENNIE
       I don't do no damn singing. Don't you
        know what hip hop is? Haven't you ever
        been to a park and listened to the ghetto
        blasters? Girl, you need to get down with
         the future. There's a whole new style that's
                  already taken over.

INT. HALLWAY TRACY'S HOUSE
MRS. MCGOVERN (Tracy's mom) is on the phone in the corridor. She is black and a former model. She has a drink in one hand and sits near a buffet table. She is talking animatedly into the receiver, either giving or receiving some juicy bit of gossip. At her feet is a neurotic Chihuahua. Enter Tracy and Kennie. The dog yaps at Kennie.

                     TRACY
                (in breeze-by mode)
                    Hi, mom.
Kennie follows Tracy into the livingroom. Mrs. McGovern does a double-take
                   on Kennie.
                 MRS. MCGOVERN
        I'll have to call you back. Her majesty
         just walked in with something she picked
                  up in the street.

INT. LIVINGROOM TRACY'S HOUSE
Kennie has never been in such a lavish home. He eyes wander around the room,

which is filled with books, photographs, art works. Mrs. McGovern enters and stares at Tracy, who ignores her and flops into a couch.

MRS. MCGOVERN
Aren't you going to introduce me to your friend?
TRACY
Umm. What did you say your name was?
KENNIE
Kennie.
TRACY
Kennie, this is my mother. She used to be a famous model.

Kennie moves to shake hands, but the dog growls and bites his sneaker.

MRS. MCGOVERN
Pee Wee, behave yourself. Tracy, can I talk to you for a minute in the kitchen please?

The women exit. Pee Wee follows them, turns around and stares and Kennie before leaving. Kennie snoops around the room but decides to move closer to the door to see if he can overhear anything being said in the kitchen.

MRS. MCGOVERN (OS)
What do you mean by bringing a street urchin into this house? Are you crazy? Wait until your father finds out about this!
TRACY (OS)
I don't know what you're getting so worked up about. He was teaching my class how to break dance.
MRS. MCGOVERN (OS)
Just go back in there, get rid of him before your father gets here, and don't bring him back.

Kennie slips back to the couch as soon as he hears footsteps in the hall. Tracy enters and sits next to him.

KENNIE
I have to get goin.
TRACY
You don't have to leave so soon.
KENNIE
That's okay.

EXT. STREET BY TRACY'S
Kennie exits the brownstone.

> TRACY
> *Hey, wait, it was really nice to meet you.*
> KENNIE
> *I just remembered I have to be somewhere.*
> TRACY
> *Wait one minute. Don't you need to write down my number?*

She runs into the brownstone and quickly re-appears with a scrap of paper and a pen. She writes her phone number on the paper and hands it to Kennie. He smiles, stuffs it in his pocket, turns and walks down the street. He looks back and sees her standing still watching him. He walks back and kisses her on the lips.
MRS. MCGOVERN'S POV on the kiss.
INT. HALLWAY TRACY'S HOUSE
Mrs. McGovern steps back from the window after she sees Kennie turn and walk away.
EXT. TRACK AT ROOSEVELT HIGH -- MORNING
A physical education class jogs out of the school building. A gym teacher waits for them at the starting line of the track. The teacher holds a clip board and a stopwatch.

> GYM TEACHER
> *Okay, first runners are Jeff Price, Charles Wilson, Mark Bussel and Kennie Shakleford...*
> CHOLLY
> *So where were you yesterday?*
> KENNIE
> *I had a date.*
> CHOLLY
> *You must be gettin serious.*
> GYM TEACHER
> *Remember, four laps. On your mark get set....go.*

The runners take off. Kennie easily sprints to the front and establishes a lead of ten steps. Cholly remains at the center of the pack. Kennie completes the first lap. The gym teacher calls out the time. Students on the sidelines are yelling encouragement.

Cholly has a determined look on his face. Although stronger than Kennie, he has never been able to beat him in a foot race. Kennie passes the chalk line.

>   GYM TEACHER
>   *One lap to go!*

 The class cheers. Cholly speeds up. Kennie round a curve and realizes another runner is gaining on him. He looks back and sees Cholly pulling alongside. Kennie smiles and speeds up.

>   KENNIE
>   *You can't take me.*

The two runners are side by side down the back stretch. We hear the CLASS YELLING. The expression on Cholly face is deadly serious. Kennie stops smiling and starts running his hardest. As they round the final curve, Cholly has pulled two steps ahead. Kennie struggles to keep up. THE CLASS IS SCREAMING. Kennie puts on a final kick and barely beats Cholly.

>   GYM TEACHER
>   *55, 4:56, 4:57...*

Cholly staggers off the track and stands with his hands on his knees. He has trouble catching his breath. Kennie walks up and looks at Cholly. He starts to say something, changes his mind and walks away.
INT. THE HEAVALO
A CLOSE SHOT shows a record spinning on a turntable. WE HEAR THE LOUD SOUNDS OF A B-BOY BREAK RECORD being cut up and scratched. A WIDER SHOT shows WHIZ KID, the fastest scratch deejay in the Bronx, as he manipulates the record. The dance floor is packed. ANGLE ON THE ENTRANCE as Kennie and Tracy enter the Heavalo. Tracy is wide-eyed with culture shock. Kennie leads her to the edge of the stage where Ramon and Cholly are standing.

>   KENNIE
>   *Meet my homeboys. Ramon. Cholly.*
>   *This is Tracy.*
>   TRACY
>   (formally shaking hands)
>   *Nice to meet you. Kennie told me*
>   *about you two.*

Ramon and Cholly greet her without enthusiasm.

RAMON
(to Kennie)
We gotta talk.

Ramon and Kenny turn away for a private conversation.

KENNIE
Bro, can't you see I'm busy right now...is this necessary?

RAMON
What is this about Atomic records?

KENNIE
Who told you bout that?

RAMON
Just bout everyone in Roosevelt been hearin bout you supposed to be gettin a deal or somethin. I just want to know if it's bullshit, like usual, you know. Also like to know why I wasn't involved in this. And Cholly been thinkin the same way.

KENNIE
First off. It ain't nutin. I dropped a tape off and never heard back nuthin. So why you two gettin so crazy paranoid and shit? Now excuse me.

Kennie takes hold of Tracy and moves her away.

CHOLLY
So what he say?

RAMON
What I tell you? He said it's all bullshit. There is no fuckin record deal, just like I tol you.

CHOLLY
He ain't cuttin us out?

RAMON
Why would he do that? It's all about the crew.

ANGLE ON THE DANCE FLOOR. Two rival break dance crews, Rock Steady and NYC Breakers, are squaring off. A fight almost breaks out as they argue over who has the freshest moves.

> CRAZY LEGS
> *We got crazy new moves! Nobody comes close!*
> GLIDEMASTER
> *I'll burn you right now, Crazy Legs.*
> CRAZY LEGS
> *Yo, you on.*

Both crews start top rocking against each other in a violent explosion of energy. A circle of spectators forms around them. A SERIES OF SHOTS show various members of each crew battling. They attack each other with invisible weapons of fury. Although they never touch each other, they do come close at times. The crowd cheers whenever they see an outstanding move. Kennie and Tracy make their way to the front of the circle.

> TRACY
> *Aren't you going to dance?*
> KENNIE
> *Those boys are too good for me.*
> TRACY
> (pushes him into circle)
> *Go Soulski, go!*

Kennie refuses to dance and heads for refuge at the bar. Tracy is disappointed, but continues to clap and watch the dancers. Only Crazy Legs and Glidemaster are left in the circle and they are taking turns breaking against each other. No longer top rocking, they are now going to the floor with back spins and hand spins. Crazy Legs wins the competion by ending with a headspin. Tracy is amazed and comes over to speak with Crazy Legs to congratulate him. Several b-boys start hitting on her immediately.

> CRAZY LEGS
> *Where you from? You from downtown? You should get down with Rock Steady Crew!*
> GLIDEMASTER
> *No, no, no! Get down with NYC Breakers. We the best, forget the rest.*
> CRAZY LEGS
> *Yo, didn't I just burn you, homey?*
> GLIDEMASTER
> *One battle does not make the war, Crazy Legs.*

A rap crew takes the stage. Everyone attention immedately shifts to crowding up against the stage to watch the rappers perform. A SERIES OF SHOTS of the rappers performing. Kennie makes peace with Tracy and they watch from the bar. He pulls her close to him. They kiss.

EXT. STREET BY TRACY'S -- NIGHT

Kennie walks Tracy home.

>   TRACY
> *What's the most important thing you want?*
>   KENNIE
> *Whata ya mean?*
>   TRACY
> *Well, if you had a lot of money, what's the first thing you'd buy?*
>   KENNIE
> *I dunno. Hah. I'd like to hand my mother a hundred thousand and say here... you never have to work again. I'd like to see her face. She don't really believe in the future of hip hop.*
>   TRACY
> *How many people in your family?*
>   KENNIE
> *Me, my moms and my little brother. I used to have an older brother but he's dead.*
>   TRACY
> *I'm so sorry. How'd it happen. I mean, is it okay to talk about?*
>   KENNIE
> *It happened two years ago. I usually don't speak on it because....well...my brother was in a gang. This was back in the day when gangs really ruled the Bronx and every project and neighborhood had a division of some gang or another. Everybody was armed, too. My brother was warlord of a Black Spades division. The Spades were the biggest and the baddest, the most feared in all the city. Divisions in almost every precinct in all three boroughs. The police decided to crack down on the gangs and since they were the biggest, they got the biggest crack-down.*

They wanted all the leaders in jail. One day they stopped his car and everybody in the car got shot. My brother got shot in nine different places with dumdum bullets to make sure he couldn't survive. And the cops ain't even supposed to use dum dum bullets. It's supposed to be against the law.
                    TRACY
            What was his name?
                    KENNIE
Everybody called him Soulski. Yeah, he was the real Soulski. But when they killed him, he had changed his mind about violence. He was becoming a peacemaker. He wanted all the gangs to change and work for positive ends. He wasn't even armed. At first, I wanted to go to war. But if you ax me, gangs are a stupid idea to begin wit. I'd much rather party, write rhymes, have fun, than watch my homies get killed in drive-bys. And now gangs coming back in style, only this time, California-style. But it's always the same crush, kill and destroy.

EXT. STOOP AT TRACY'S BROWNSTONE

                    TRACY
    *My mother used to be a model.
    That's how she met my father.*
                    KENNIE
    Your father's white, right?
                    TRACY
        How'd you know?
                    KENNIE
    Believe me, it's obvious.
                    TRACY
My dad's a photographer. He makes a lot of money flying around the world shooting advertisements for major corporations. He photographed my mother one day

> *and that's how they met. Then my mother started to lose her looks, which just made her drink more, which kind of leads to a snowball effect, I think. She might even blame her downfall on me, pregancy can have a debilitating effect on modeling careers.*

KENNIE
> *You shouldn't talk like that about your moms.*

TRACY
> *What time is it anyway? I should probably go inside before the sun comes up and she sees me out here talking to her least favorite person in the world.*

Tracy stands and opens the door. Kennie kisses her. And then follows her into the brownstone. They tip-toe up the stairs.

KENNIE
> *Where's your parent's room?*

TRACY
> *Shhh! I'm on the top floor, there's an entire floor between us. I moved up there for the privacy.*
> *As they pass the first floor, Pee Wee darts out from the parent's bedroom and starts yapping at Kennie.*

TRACY
> *Pee Wee, shhh...*

Tracy picks up the dog and strokes him to calm him down while silently urging Kennie to continue tip-toeing up the steps.

MRS. MCGOVERN (OS)
> *Is that you Tracy?*

TRACY
> *Go back to sleep mom.*

INT. TRACY'S BEDROOM

KENNIE
> *Where's the fire escape just in case?*

TRACY

> *Right through that window.*

Kennie opens the window and mentally checks out his escape route.

KENNIE
*What would your father do if he caught
me up here?*

TRACY
I guess he'd shoot you.
(pause)
*Just kidding. He doesn't even have a gun.
My father's not the violent type.*

KENNIE
*How many boys been up in this room
before me?*

TRACY
Aren't we the snoopy one?

They kiss and fall into bed. Kennie kicks off his sneakers. Pee Wee approaches the sneakers, sniffs them, and then pees on them while Kennie and Tracy make love.

EXT. TRACY'S BROWNSTONE -- DAWN

Kennie pokes his head out the window. He looks disheveled. He carries his sneakers in one hand as he makes his way silently down the fire espace. He has to jump the last floor onto a concrete pad with bare feet. He winces in pain, recovers and then hurries down the street before he is spotted by someone.

EXT. CENTRAL PARK -- DAY

A VARIETY OF SHOTS show Tracy taking Kenny on a tour of her favorite spots in Central Park. The MUSIC SWELLS.

EXT. SOUTH BRONX -- DAY

Kennie takes Tracy on a tour of the South Bronx. He introduces her to people on the street. They pass by a movie theater advertising a Kung Fu film with subtitles. They visit a local artist's studio and watch a plaster cast made of a kid's face. The studio is filled with faces from the South Bronx.

EXT. DOWNTOWN -- DAY

Tracy takes Kennie on a tour of Soho. The visit an art gallery.

INT. OFF BROADWAY THEATER

Kennie sits in the audience at the back of the room while Tracy auditions.

EXT. PHONE BOOTH -- DAY

Kennie is standing at a pay phone and holding a slip of paper. We hear a PHONE RINGING.

INT. ATOMIC RECORDS RECEPTION ROOM

                    HOWIE
                   Atomic.
        EXT. PHONE BOOTH -- DAY
               Is Mr. Bither in?
                    HOWIE
                Who's calling?
                   KENNIE
                   Soulski.
                    HOWIE
              You left a tape here?
                   KENNIE
                    Yeah.
                    HOWIE
              He hasn't heard it yet.
                   KENNIE
         *How long is this gonna take? I dropped it
                off two weeks ago and...*

We hear a CLICK and the line goes dead.
EXT. STREET BY KENNIE'S

                   CHOLLY
            *If it wasn't for you we'd still be down
           with Theodore's system. We never practice
            anymore cause your always hanging with
                 your rich bitch girl friend...*
                   KENNIE
                 What cho say?
                   CHOLLY
                You heard me sucka.
                    RAMON
           Yo, why don't you both chill out!
                   KENNIE
             Don't be calling her a bitch.
                   CHOLLY
          Yeah, whatcha gonna do about it?
Kennie pushes Cholly. Cholly pushes back harder. Ramon tries to intercede.
Kennie swings at Cholly, but Cholly catches his fist in his hand. Ramon breaks
                   them apart.
                   CHOLLY

                      215

                    (to Ramon)
            I'm through with this shit.
                Cholly walks away.
                        RAMON
            Why you have to start that?
                        KENNIE
        I started it? Why is he acting so crazy?

EXT. RIVERSIDE PARK -- SUNSET
Kennie and Tracy are leaning on a railing, looking at the Hudson River. The George Washington Bridge is visible in the distance.

                        KENNIE
                So what did you tell them?
                        TRACY
            I said I was going out with Lisa.
                        KENNIE
                What if they call her?
                        TRACY
        She knows what to say. She's my best friend.
                        KENNIE
        They ain't never ever gonna accept me.
                        TRACY
            They just don't know you. That's all.
                        KENNIE
            I guess I AM a bad influence.
                        TRACY
        *Are you crazy? You're the best influence
                        I have.*

EXT. STREET BY HARDWARE STORE -- DAY
Kennie and Ramon walk down the street. Ramon wears a large overcoat that is rigged to carry stolen cans of paint.

                        KENNIE
            Make sure you get some Fed Purple.
                        RAMON
                If they have any left.
They stop in front of the hardware store display window and survey the spray

paint cans on display.
KENNIE
Check it out: electric rasberry.
RAMON
Where's the clerk?
KENNIE
At the counter.
RAMON
Just one guy?
KENNIE
No the manager is in the back. He's the one to watch out for.

INT. HARDWARE STORE

Kennie enters and walks up to the counter. Ramon enters a few beats behind him and heads for the spray-paint section. Kennie approaches the counter.

KENNIE
I'm lookin for a paint brush.
CLERK
For what kind of paint?

Ramon loads cans of spray paint into the hidden pockets sewn in the inside of his coat.

KENNIE
(inspecting brush)
Do you have anything bigger?

The clerk turns around and picks another brush off the wall behind him. He hands the brush to Kennie, who seems distracted. The clerk gets suspicious and looks around the room. He catches sight of Ramon in a mirror, ducking down behind the spray paint display. He runs over to see what Ramon is doing.

CLERK
Can I help you? Are you two together?
KENNIE
Huh? Can I get some help with this brush I want to buy?
CLERK
(to Ramon)
We don't sell spraypaint to anyone under 18. So unless you got an ID, stay away from this section.
RAMON
I was just leaving anyway.

Ramon trys to casually walk out of the door, but his coat is overloaded with spray paint cans and they clank togeter and he waddles away from the Clerk. The Clerk runs after Ramon, who speeds up and heads for the door.

KENNIE
*Okay, I changed my mind. Here's
your paint brush.*

Kennie throws the brush on the counter and also heads for the door. The Clerk grabs Ramon by the collar. He struggles. Kennie tries to push the Clerk away. Two paint cans fall out of Ramon's coat and hit the floor.

CLERK
Put it back!
RAMON
Okay. Okay.

The struggle ends in a momentary truce. Ramon picks up the cans of paint and suddenly takes off running, accidently bumping into a battery display, knocking batteries everywhere. Kennie and Ramon exit with the Clerk hot on their heels.
EXT. HARDWARE STORE
Kennie and Ramon run for their lives. Paint cans accidentally eject from Ramon's coat every few steps, but as he loses paint, Ramon is able to run faster. The Clerk
cannot keep up.
INT. DANCE THEATER OF HARLEM
Tracy drops off her application.
EXT. ATOMIC RECORDS STOREFRONT -- DAY
Kennie enters the office.
INT. ATOMIC RECORDS RECEPTION ROOM
KENNIE'S POV. The reception room is deserted. On the left is
Bither's office. On the right is a low-budget recording studio. A red light marked "RECORDING" is on. Kennie snoops around the office. The door to the studio opens and Howie appears.

HOWIE
Whata you want?
KENNIE
*I left a tape here. I got a message
from my moms that you called me
yesterday.*
HOWIE
*Oh yeah. Soulski, right? Here you
go.*

Howie fishes around in the desk, finds Kennie's tape and hands it back to him.

Kennie is befuddled. He states at the tape in his hand.
>   HOWIE
>   *Yeah, he passed. Not commercial*
>   *enough.*
>   KENNIE
>   *He really listened to it?*
>   HOWIE
>   *It's not what he's looking for, okay?*

EXT. ATOMIC RECORDS STOREFRONT -- DAY
Kennie exits the building. He walks a block, stops and hurls the tape against a brick wall, shattering it.
INT. HALLWAY TRACY'S HOUSE
Mrs. McGovern is on the phone. He hear THE FRONT DOOR SLAM. Tracy walks by. Mrs. McGovern grabs her arm and points at at letter on the buffet table. INSERT on the letter: an official envelope from the Dance Theater of Harlem. Tracy picks up the letter and walks upstairs.
INT. TRACY'S BEDROOM
A close shot on the torn envelope on the floor.
A WIDER ANGLE shows Tracy frantically dialing a phone number. She has the letter in her hand.
CUT TO:
INT. HALLWAY KENNIE'S HOUSE
We hear the PHONE RINGING. Lee answers it.

>   LEE
>   *Hello. Just a minute.*
>   (shouts)
>   *Hey, Kennie. Some girl on the phone*
>   *for you.*

Kennie opens the door to his bedroom and moves slowly down the hall.
>   KENNIE
>   *Hello.*
>   TRACY
>   *Guess what!*
>   KENNIE
>   *What?*
>   TRACY
>   *I got in! I made it!*
>   KENNIE
>   *Huh?*
>   TRACY

    I'm an apprentice member of the
    Dance Theater of Harlem.
            KENNIE
        That's great.
            TRACY
    You don't sound very excited.
            KENNIE
    It's fuckin great. Whata you want
        me to say?
            TRACY
    Well, don't you think we should
        celebrate?
            KENNIE
    I'm kinda busy right now.
            TRACY
       What's the matter?
            KENNIE
Nuthin. I just been thinkin it over you
know. I don't know if you and me are
such a good idea. I mean, you know
    how your parents feel.
            TRACY
You really think I care what they think?
            KENNIE
    That's just the thing. Maybe you
       should listen to them.
            TRACY

    Don't use my parents as some lame
      excuse to get what you want.

            KENNIE
    Look you're gonna be super busy now.
      It's not working out between us.
            TRACY
        So this is it?
            KENNIE
        I guess so.

We hear a CLICK. Tracy has hung up the phone. Kennie stares at the receiver. He hangs up the phone and walks toward his room. His movements are slow and methodical.

INT. KENNIE'S BEDROOM -- NIGHT
Kennie sits on the bed. He stares at a flyer for a show at the Heavalo. He sits calmly for a while. Suddenly, Kennie reaches over, rips the flyer off the wall and crumples it into a ball and throws it in the corner. He goes into the closet and gets out his paint stash.

EXT. STREET BY RAMON'S -- NIGHT
Kennie's messenger bag is bulging with paint. He turns the corner, stops and knocks on the window of a first floor apartment. The window opens and Ramon appears.

> RAMON
> *Wussup?*

We hear the sound of A MAN YELLING IN SPANISH and the sound of a TV SET TURNED UP from inside the apartment.

> KENNIE
> *What's goin on?*
> RAMON
> *Nuthin. My dumb sister is pregnant again and the old man is yellin at her.*
> KENNIE
> *Who the daddy this time?*
> RAMON
> *She ain't sayin'. Maybe she's not sure.*
> KENNIE
> *You ready to throw up that whole train tribute?*
> RAMON
> *Right now?*
> KENNIE
> *You always talkin about doin a full train masterpiece. Well, I finally got the paint together.*
> RAMON
> *Jus give me a second to get dressed. I'll meet you out front.*

EXT. ELEVATED TRAIN TRACKS -- NIGHT
A train splattered with graffiti roars by. The CAMERA PANS to the ground,

where Kennie and Ramon are running. The soundtrack SWELLS.
EXT. SUBWAY STATION
Kennie and Ramon race up the stairs to the platform.
INT. SUBWAY CAR
Kennie and Ramon ride a subway downtown. They get off at Chambers Street.
INT. SUBWAY STATION
They walk to the end of the platform, jump down on the tracks and start running through the tunnel.
INT. SUBWAY TUNNEL
The run along the dark tunnel.
KENNIE'S POV. Several lights are visible on the track ahead. Kennie slows down, grabs Ramon's arm and points to the lights.

> RAMON
> *What is it?*
> KENNIE
> *Transit workers.*
> RAMON
> *Shit.*
> KENNIE
> *We'll go this way and work our way around.*
> *The layup is just south of here.*
> RAMON
> *You sure?*
> KENNIE
> *Pretty sure.*

They cross several tracks and hug the wall of the tunnel. KENNIE'S POV. Three transit workers are sharingk a quart of beer. Bathed in yellow light form the laterns, the workers are partially hidden by the pillars of the tunnel. Kennie keeps his eyes on the workers as he moves with his back against the wall. A train rumbles down the track. Kennie and Ramon press close to the wall as the train passes. Kennie accidently kicks a bottle onto the track. We hear THE BOTTLE BREAK.

> TRANSIT WORKER
> *What was that?*

The Transit Worker shines a high-powered flashlight into the tunnel.

> TRANSIT WORKER 2
> *Who's there?*

> TRANSIT WORKER
> *Must be a rat.*
> The light shines on Kennie and Ramon.
> TRANSIT WORKER 3
> *That ain't no rat. It's two goddam
> graffiti writers.*
> TRANSIT WORKER
> *Get em.*

The three workers charge across the track. Kennie and Ramon run. A SERIES OF ANGLES show the chase through the tunnels. Kennie and Ramon run through a maze of interconnecting tunnels and quickly lose their bearings.

> RAMON
> *Which way?*
> KENNIE
> *I dunno.*
> RAMON
> *They still behind us?*
> KENNIE'S POV. Three flashlights in the distance are moving closer.
> KENNIE
> *Yeah. This way!*

Kennie runs into an old, out-of-service tunnel. The walls are crumbling brick. Kennie and Ramon splash through several mud puddles. A rat scurries across their path. The tunnel gets smaller. Kennie and Ramon bend over and keep running. The tunnel grows darker until nothing is visible.

> RAMON
> (panic-stricken)
> *Yo, Kennie! Where are you?*
> KENNIE
> *Right here.*
> RAMON
> *Let's go back. I can't see
> anything.*
> KENNIE
> *There's a light ahead.*

Kennie emerges from the tunnel into a lighted area and collapses against a wall. Ramon emerges and collapses next to him.

> KENNIE
> *Think we lost them?*

>   RAMON
>   *I dunno. Where are we?*
> KENNIE'S POV as he scans the area. Fifty feet away, parked on a lay-up and obscured by the pillars, is the white train. THE MUSIC SWELLS.
>   KENNIE
>   *Look!*
>   RAMON
>   *Oh my god!*

THE CAMERA PANS the spotless sides of the train. ANOTHER ANGLE shows Kennie and Ramon as they reverently approach the train. Ramon runs his hands along the virgin surface on the train. Kennie unpacks his paint.

>   KENNIE
>   *I know this layup. The "D" train*
>   *runs on the other side.*

Ramon puts a fatcap on a can of paint. He sprays an outline on the train.

>   RAMON
>   *Fill that. I'll work the other side.*

Kennie uses the can with the fatcap to fill in the outline Ramon created. Ramon grabs the sack filled with paint. He crawls under the car and emerges on the other side. Kennie continues painting. Ramon unpacks his supplies.
TIME LAPSE:
Kennie and Ramon have filled nine of the cars with paintings and are working on the last one. Their ten-car masterpiece is almost finished. The designs in Ramon's sketchbook have come vibrantly to life. They are working on the last car, and most of it has been outlined already. Kennie and Ramon are filling in the outlines with the fat-capped cans.
CUT TO:
INT. SUBWAY TUNNEL
A subway train is headed towards the layup. Ramon is spraying another outline. He sets the can down. INSERT on the can, which has a nozzle frozen open that sprays a tiny mist of paint. Ramon doesn't notice the defective nozzle. He continues painting. The subway train enters the lay-up without slowing down. Kennie hears the train, looks up, but doesn't pay much attention. The train is running on the track next to Ramon. The track has a slight curve. As the train rounds the curve, it throws up a shower of sparks. The paint can is ignited by

the sparks. We hear an EXPLOSION. The first explosion is followed by another, larger EXPLOSION as other cans are ignited. The second EXPLOSION sets off a BRILLIANT FLASH. Kennie sees the flash. We hear Ramon SCREAM. Kennie drops his can and crawls under the car. Ramon is on fire. He runs down the tunnel. Kennie chases Ramon, yelling for him to stop running. He finally catches him and puts the fire out with his jacket.
EXT. STREET -- NIGHT
It is raining and the streets are already slick with water. Kennie and Ramon emerge from a subway station. Kennie supports Ramon, who is obviously in shock. Ramon's skin is hanging in sheets from his face. His hair is burnt. Kennie hails a cab. It slows while the driver looks at Kennie, then Ramon. The driver pulls away without stopping. Kennie keeps trying to hail a cab. A gypsy cab finally pulls over. The driver is a Rasta from Jamaica.

>   RASTA
>   *Mon, what happened to you?*
>   KENNIE
>   *Can you take us to a hospital?*
>   RASTA
>   *Get in mon, get in.*

EXT. STREET -- NIGHT
The cab hurtles down the street.
INT. GYPSY CAB
Kennie looks at Ramon, grimmaces and turns his face away.
EXT. STREET -- NIGHT
The cab careens through an intersection.
INT. GYPSY CAB
The Rasta honks his horn as he barrels thorugh a red light.
EXT. HOSPITAL EMERGENCY DRIVE
The cab squeals into the hospital driveway. Kennie opens the door and slowly helps Ramon out. The Rasta runs into the hospital and returns with two orderlies pushing a stretcher.
INT. EMERGENCY ROOM
The doctor on duty opens Ramons mouth and checks his throat for signs of swelling. Kennie wanders into the room. A nurse grabs him.

>   KENNIE
>   *That's my best friend.*
>   NURSE
>   *You have to wait outside.*

INT. WAITING ROOM
Kennie takes a seat. The hospital burn specialist runs down the hallway and enters the emergency room. The nurse at the reception desk waves at Kennie. Kennie walks over to her.

>NURSE
>*You're with the boy who got burned?*
>*What's his name?*
>KENNIE
>*Ramon Franco*
>NURSE
>*Address?*
>KENNIE
>*167th Street, Bronx.*
>NURSE
>*What address?*
>KENNIE
>*I dunno. It's the gray building on*
>*the corner of Webster and 167th.*

INT. EMERGENCY ROOM
The burn specialist consults with the emergency room doctor, while a nurse removes Ramon's clothes with a sissors.

>SPECIALIST
>*Is the airway clear?*
>DOCTOR
>*Doesn't seem to be swelling. Should*
>*we tube him anyway?*
>SPECIALIST
>(to Nurse)
>*Start the I.V.*
>(to Doctor)
>*I'd like to get him into the tank*
>*room as soon as possible.*

INT. HOSPITAL CORRIDOR
A hospital bed is wheeled out of the emergency room. Ramon lies unconscious on the bed, a sheet draped over him. An I.V. needle is attached to his arm. The receptionist continues questioning Kennie. Kennie sees Ramon, breaks off the conversation and follows the hospital bed into the elevator.

INT. BURN CENTER
Ramon is wheeled into the tank room. Ramon is loaded onto a metal platform and his wounds are debearded. Two nurses dress the body. When they are done, Ramon is covered in bandages.
INT. HOSPITAL CORRIDOR
Kennie waits. He sighs. He leans back. He props his head against the wall. Ramon is wheeled out of the tank room and placed into a hospital room in intensive care. A CLOSE SHOT on Kennie, who has fallen asleep in his chair. A white body walks over to him. A hand gently nudges Kennie's shoulder. Kennie opens his eyes.

NURSE
*Your friend is awake. Do you want
to see him?*

Kennie nods his head.
INT. HOSPITAL ROOM
The nurse leads Kennie to Ramon's bed and exits. Ramon's bandaged arm slowly raises. Kennie sits by the bed.

RAMON
Bro, I thought you left me.
KENNIE
Be serious, homey.
RAMON
*Just don't tell the old man how this
happened.*
KENNIE
*Don't worry. We just have to keep
our stories straight.*
RAMON
(laughs)
*Look at me. I look like a fuckin
mummy. Where's Cholly? He should be
here to see this.*
(wheezing for air)
*Whenever something stupid happens,
he's always....*

                    KENNIE
              Don't talk. Just rest.

Ramon is unable to catch his breath. His vocal chords are collapsing from the burns. He wheezes. His face turns blue. Kennie looks around helplessly. An alarm next to the bed goes off.

                    KENNIE
                  Help! Help!

The burn specialist runs into the room. He is followed by a nurse wheeling a respirator. The specialist places the respirator over Ramon's mouth, but Ramon fights the machine instead of breathing with it. Ramon suffocates. Kennie is ushered out of the room by a nurse.

                   SPECIALIST
            I told them to check the airway...

INT. HOSPITAL CORRIDOR
Kennie drifts aimlessly down the hall. THE CAMERA PANS to the window. The sun is rising.
EXT. ELEVATED TRAIN TRACKS -- DAWN
The ten-car masterpiece painted by Ramon and Kennie crosses the Bronx. There aren't many people on the street, but the few that see it are amazed. A photographer snaps a photo of the train.
EXT. SUBWAY YARD -- DAY
Three transit workers are preparing the buffing machine that removes graffiti from the sides of subway cars.

                  TRANSIT WORKER
           Hey, we got a fresh one. Just taken
                out of service and sent over
              because the paint was still wet.
                  TRANSIT WORKER 2
                Must have got hit last night.

A CLOSE SHOT shows the side of the train slowly entering the buffing machine. A CLOSE SHOT shows the jets of toxic solvent spraying on the side of the train, smearing and obliterating the murals that Ramon and Kennie worked so hard on. The train emerges from the buffing machine. It has turned into an ugly mud color as all the paint has smeared together.
EXT. PLAYGROUND -- DAY

Several full-court games are in progress.
ANOTHER ANGLE. Kennie and Lee are playing on a small side-court. Kennie easily dribbles around his brother. He dribbles inside and then outside. He takes a long shot, which misses. Lee grabs the rebound and dribbles toward the basket. Kennie pretends to guard Lee, but let's him get by. Lee shoots a layup. The ball bounces around the rim and goes in. Lee WHOOPS with joy. Kennie smiles.

KENNIE
Nice shot.
LEE
Eight to four. You ain't gotta chance now.
KENNIE
(dribbling)
You shouldn't have said that. Now I'll have to crush you.

Kennie easily dribbles around Lee, leaps up and trys to dunk the ball. However, he comes up barely short and the ball carooms off the back of the rim. It flys into Lee's hands. Lee quickly throws up a shot and it goes in.

LEE
Ten. I win!
KENNIE
Uh-uh. You forget to take it back so it's my score. Six eight, and I'm about to break.

Kennie dribbles around Lee and goes for a lay-up. He does this again and declares himself the winner. A WIDER ANGLE shows LONNIE approaching.

LONNIE
Yo, Kennie, wussup, mellow? Where you been? I haven't seen you in a long time, man.
KENNIE
Same ol, same ol.
LONNIE
You haven't been down at the Heavalo? Hey, man, I'm so sorry to hear about what happened to Ramon. I heard about it. That was really sad, man. And he had such a fresh style on the turntables, besides being one of the dopest fuckin writers of

>   *this era. So you heard what's up with Cholly?*
>   KENNIE
>   *What?*
>   LONNIE
>   *He's down wit the Casanovas.*
>   Lee throws the ball to Kennie. Kennie passes it back.
>   LONNIE
>   *Well, I gotta fly. It was good to*
>   *see you, bro.*
>   KENNIE
>   *Catch you later.*
>   Kennie takes a shot and retrieves the ball.
>   LEE
>   *How come you don't go to the*
>   *Heavalo no more?*

Kennie takes a shot and does not answer.
INT. DANCE THEATER OF HARLEM
A dozen dancers, dressed in warm-ups, are facing the INSTRUCTOR, who demonstrates an exercise, and they watches the class repeat it. Tracy is on the end of the line, and she seems distracted.
INSTRUCTOR
Tracy, if you're going to do it like that,
you might as well not do it at all.
One more time, just Tracy and me.
Tracy struggles to master the exercise.
EXT. STREET BY TRACY'S
Tracy listlessly walks home. She stops at the corner. A b-boy carrying a ghetto blaster passes by going the opposite direction. Tracy glances at the b-boy, for a minute she thought that might be Kennie coming to apologize.
INT. DINING ROOM TRACY'S HOUSE
Tracy and her parents eat dinner. Tracy picks at her food.

>   MR. MCGOVERN
>   *He wants me to do more editorial*
>   *work. I told him there's no money*
>   *in that anymore. I could get a*
>   *catalogue but I'm sick of doing*
>   *catalogues.*
>   MRS. MCGOVERN
>   *Tracy, will you eat your food and*
>   *stop pushing it around your plate?*

                    TRACY
                I'm not hungry.

Tracy's parents share a concerned look.
EXT. ROOSEVELT HIGH SCHOOL
Smitty, Cholly and the Casanovas are hanging out after school. Smitty is demonstrating his stick-up technique.

                    SMITTY
        Wait until he's almost past and
        then come up on both sides. Press
        him into the side of a parked car.
Smitty presses Casanovav 1 against the building. Cholly stands behind him.
                CASANOVA 1
            (acting like a white man)
                    Eeek!
                    SMITTY
                    (laughs)
        Naw. Not like that. They give a real worried
        expression--like you're gonna stab them.
        You just say, Okay, motherfucker. Open your
            pockets or face the consequences.

KENNIE'S POV on Cholly and the Casanovas. He crosses the sreet to avoid them.
INT. HELENE'S BEDROOM -- NIGHT
Helene sits in bed. She wears glasses and reads a paperback romance novel. Kennie stands in the doorway.

                    KENNIE
                    Hi.
                    HELENE
                How are you?
                    KENNIE
            Pretty good. What ya reading?
                    HELENE
            It's just a silly story. Nothing
                    important.
                    KENNIE
                Is it good, though?
                    HELENE

It's okay.
Kennie turns to leave.

Kennie?

KENNIE
Yeah?

HELENE
Come over here for a minute will you? Sit down on the bed. Is everything all right?

KENNIE
Yeah.

HELENE
How's school? Have you been doing all your homework?

KENNIE
It don't really hold my full interest no more, to tell the truth, mom.

HELENE
And why is that?

KENNIE
I dunno. Most of it doesn't seem all that useful, interesting or even worth caring about. Who cares if you can memorize a bunch of facts, anyway?

HELENE
You know, Kennie. I was just thinking the other day that this family has been through an awful lot. The move to New York was so difficult. Everyone seemed so strange here at first. I thought I'd never find work. Then your father left us, and I didn't know how I was going to survive. We almost moved back to North Carolina to live with Gramma Tyler. Would you have preferred that?

KENNIE

> *No way. I mean. She's all right.*
> *But it's kinda boring down there*
> *compared to the Bronx.*

                    HELENE
> *Well, I couldn't raise the bus fare*
> *at the time and Lee was less than a*
> *year old....But then your brother*
> *died. I never told you. But that*
> *almost took the life out of me. For*
> *a long time I had no desire for*
> *much of anything. And no pleasure*
> *either. I couldn't work very well.*
> *I didn't care about eating. I*
> *couldn't get a good night's sleep.*
> *I almost lost faith. I almost gave*
> *up. But I forced myself. For you*
> *and Lee. I never thought that pain*
> *would pass. But it did. Now I*
> *realize we never lost your brother*
> *because I see him every day in you.*
> *Somehow, he handed down the good*
> *things in himself to you. And in*
> *that same way I think Ramon will*
> *always be with us. You understand?*
> *The MOST important thing is to go*
> *on.*

Kennie bows his head and Helene hugs him.
EXT. STREET BY HEAVALO
A MOVING SHOT of the view from the window of a taxi.
INT. TAXI
Tracy and Lisa are in the back seat.

                    LISA
> *Are you sure we're going the right*
> *way?*

The taxi drives past a bombed-out building.

                    TRACY
> *Oh shit. I just realized, what if*
> *he's with some other girl?*

The cab pulls to a stop in front of the Heavalo, which has a small crowd standing outside. The crowd stares at the young white girl in the cab.

                    LISA
         Traaa-cy? Are you sure this is the
           place? This doesn't look too good
                    to me.
But Tracy is not paying attention to her friend's fears. She has already departed the cab and gotten into line.
         Oh, wait for me then. Oh my god.

Lisa pays the taxi driver and exits the cab. She gets in line behind Tracy and they slowly work their way into the club.
INT. THE HEAVALO
Tracy searches through the crowd. Kool Herc presides over the deejay platform. The dance floor is filled with b-boys and b-girls. Lisa follows Tracy on her search. A b-boy approaches her and asks her to dance.

                    LISA
          I'm just here with my friend. I
            actually don't belong here?
TRACY'S POV on Cholly and Smitty with their backs against the bar. Tracy approaches them.
                   TRACY
          Cholly! I'm so glad I found you? Is
                  Kennie here?
                   CHOLLY
            Hi Tracy. I haven't seen Kennie at
            the Heavalo in weeks. When's the
            last time Kennie was down here?
                   SMITTY
           Not since Ramon got wasted.
                   TRACY
              What's that mean?
                   CHOLLY
              You know Ramon?
                   TRACY
            Of course I know him.
                   CHOLLY
          Well, he ain't wit us no more. He
            died in a graffiti accident. I

> believe it may have been Kennie's
> fault and that may be why we don't
> see him no more.

                    TRACY
> Can you take me to his house, or
> give me his address?

                    SMITTY
> We havin a party after the show
> tonight? Want some coke?

EXT. THE HEAVALO

Tracy and Lisa emerge from the club. A b-boy hands them a flyer. INSERT ON THE FLYER. The Heavalo Rap Throwdown. Show you face in the place for the MC competition. Best act wins a record with StreetWise Records. Sponsored by StreetWise Productions. $5.

                    LISA
> How we going to get home?

                    TRACY
                  (to b-boy)
> How far is the nearest subway?

INT. CASANOVA BASE HOUSE

Cholly is seen getting fully fucked up on base. Smitty and the rest of the Casanovas are also doing hits, drinking malt liquor and playing with their weapons. They are taking turns on a girl in the bedroom. Smitty shows something to Cholly.

                    SMITTY
> You know what this is? It's called
> crack! We don't have to cook base
> no mo. You can put this straight
> into a pipe and smoke it.

                    CHOLLY
> Wow. What's this go for?

                    SMITTY
> About five dollars a hit. This shit
> is gonna take over. Cholly, I
> forget to tell you. We have a
> little induction ceremony for you.
> It's time to make your bones with
> the Casanovas.

                    CASANOVA !
> Where to?

                        SMITTY
                I know a place that is ripe.

INT. BODEGA
An Arab is behind the counter at an all-night convenience store. WE HEAR A
BELL RING. A customer enters and buys a quart of beer. The man behind the
counter takes his money, bags the bottle and give him his change. ANGLE ON
THE DOOR. Cholly enters. THE BELL OVER THE DOOR RINGS. Cholly
stops at the potato chip display. A CLOSE SHOT on Cholly's torso. He opens
his coat. The butt end of a pistol is sticking out of his belt. THE BELL RINGS.
ANGLE ON THE DOOR as Smitty and two Casanovas enter. The Arab is
immediately concerned. The Casanovas go straight to the beer section and start
racking up cases to go. Cholly picks out one bag of potato chips and puts it on
the counter with a $20 bill. When the Arab takes the money, he flashes the gun.

                        CHOLLY
                *You know what this is so don't do
                nutin stupid. Put all your money in
                            the bag.*
After the Arab puts some money in the bag Cholly looks at him in anger.

                *That's it? Give me the stash or I
                    swear to god, I'll blow your
                        motherfuckin head off.*

The Arab produces some big bills stashed under the register
drawer.
EXT. BODEGA -- NIGHT
The Casanova's run out loaded down with beer and jump into a waiting car.
Cholly is the last to exit. He backs out with the gun in one hand and the money
in the other. He jumps into the car.
INT. CASANOVA CAR
They all laugh riotously as the car peels away from the curb and careens down
the street. Smitty sticks his gun out the window and fires off a round into the
window of the bodega.
EXT. STREET BY KENNIE'S -- DAY
Tracy walks down the street. She opens her bag and removes a scrap of paper
to check. She consults the paper and checks the address of the building she is in
front of. Tracy enters the building.
INT. HALLWAY KENNIE'S HOUSE
Tracy passes the superintendent, who is cleaning graffiti marks off the wall.

Tracy stands before a door. She takes a deep breath and knocks. She waits, knocks again louder. The door opens a crack. Lee opens the door.

> TRACY
> *Hi. Is Kennie home?*
> LEE
> *No, he ain't here.*
> TRACY
> *You expect him back soon?*
> LEE
> *Not really.*
> TRACY
> *You're Lee, right?*
> LEE
> *Maybe, who are you?*
> TRACY
> *I'm a friend of your brother's from Manhattan. Can I come in?*
> LEE
> *I ain't supposed to let nobody in.*
> TRACY
> *Well, I ain't nobody and this is very important to me. I'd just like to talk to you for a minute.*

INT. KENNIE'S BEDROOM -- DAY
Lee and Tracy are seated. Tracy is leafing through Kennie's latest book of raps.

> LEE
> *See, he still writing raps. He just not performing them outloud no mo.*
> TRACY
> (reading)
> *These are amazing.*
> LEE
> *Yeah, it's good stuff.*

WE HEAR THE SOUND OF A DOOR OPENING AND FOOTSTEPS. Enter Kennie.

KENNNIE
What's goin on here? Is that my notebook?

EXT. ECHO PARK -- DAY
Kennie and Tracy are seated on a bench.

KENNIE
We started out playing free jams here on Saturday afternoons. See that streetlight? We used to kick out the bottom and hotwire Theodore's system to it. I almost got electrocuted more than once.

TRACY
Did you see this flyer? This show looks perfect for you.

KENNIE
Yeah, except I ain't really a rapper no more.

TRACY
What are you talking about? Some of those raps in your book are better than anything I've ever heard from you.

KENNIE
But it's all too lowdown and depressin. Nobody wants to hear that depressin shit.

TRACY
You are wrong. The real story is way way better than talking about cars, money and egos. Why don't you just give this audition a shot and see what happens? I mean, what's the worst that can happen?

KENNIE
I wrote most of it for a duo. Supposed to have a lot of back and forth.

TRACY
So? Where's Cholly?

KENNIE
I haven't seen him since the funeral.

*Besides he down wit the Casanova's
now. I don't know if he would even want to.*
             TRACY
    Well, maybe you should ask him?

EXT. THE HEAVALO -- NIGHT
A long line of people is stretched around the corner, waiting to get in.
INT. THE HEAVALO
WE HEAR THE SOUND SYSTEM BLASTING. A dozen crews and individual rappers are lined up near the stage, waiting to perform. Kool Herc presides over the line of performers. He holds a clipboard with a list. Frosty and Mel stand on the stage. They are dressed in their stage costumes. Kennie and Cholly are dressed in their usual clothes.

             KOOL HERC
    *Are we ready to start the great
         emcee throwdown?*

The crowd applauds. A VARIETY OF SHOTS on the contestants performing rap routines. Kennie and Cholly take the stage with little fanfare.

             KOOL HERC
    And now for Soulski and Cholly.

The deejay starts the beat. Kennie and Cholly recite *The Message* originally written by Melle Mel [Note from author: I do not claim copyright over the following lyrics which are taken from the Message originally published by Sugarhill Records.]

              KENNIE
    *Broken glass everywhere, people
     pissing on the stairs, you know
          they just don't care.*
              CHOLLY
    *I can't take the smell, I can't
     take the noise, got no money to
     move out, I guess I got no choice.*
              KENNIE
    *Rats in the front room, roaches in
     the back. Junkies in the alley with*
              KENNIE
    a baseball bat. I tried to get

away, but I couldn't get far cause the man with the tow-truck repossessed my car.
CHOLLY
Don't push me, cause I'm close to the edge. I'm tryin not to lose my head. It's like a jungle sometimes, it makes me wonder how I keep from going under.
KENNIE
My brother said Soulski, I don't wanna go to school cause the teacher's a jerk, he must think I'm a fool. And all the kids smoke reefer, I think it'd be cheaper if I just got a job, learned to be a street sweeper. I dance to the beat, shuffle my feet. Wear a shirt and tie and run with the creeps.
CHOLLY
Cause it's all about money, ain't a damn thing funny, you got to have a con in this land of milk and honey. I can't walk through the park, cause it's crazy after the dark. Keep my hand on the gun, cause they got me on the run. I feel like an outlaw, broke my last glass jaw. Hear them say you want some more, livin on a seesaw.
KENNIE
A child was born, with no state of mind. Blind to the ways of mankind. God is smiling on you but he's frownin too, cause only God knows what you go through. You grow in the ghetto, living second rate. And your eyes will sing a song of deep hate. The places you play and where you stay, looks like one great big alley way. You'll admire all the number book takers, thugs, pimps,

> *pushers and the big money makers.*
> *Driving big cars, spending twenties*
> *and tens. And you wanna grow up to*
> *be just like them.*

CHOLLY

> *Smugglers, scrambles, burglars,*
> *gamblers pickpockets, peddlers and*
> *even pan-handlers. You say I'm*
> *cool, I'm no fool but then you wind*
> *up droppin out of high school. Now*
> *youre unemployed, all null 'n void.*
> *Walking around like you're Pretty*
> *Boy Floyd. Turned stickup kid, look*
> *what you done did. Got sent up for*
> *a eight-year bid.*

KENNIE

> *Now your manhood is took and you're*
> *a maytag. Spend the next two years*
> *as an undercover fag. Being used*
> *and abused, and served like hell.*
> *'Till one day you was find hung*
> *dead in a cell. It was plain to see*
> *that your life was lost. You was*
> *cold and your body swung back and*
> *forth. But now your eyes sing the*
> *sad sad song of how you lived so*
> *fast and died so young.*

VARIOUS ANGLES on the crowd, which is amazed by the realism and intensity of the rap. CLOSE ON TRACY, standing next to Helene. They are both into the music. PAN TO LEE, standing nearby. The audience applauds, Kool Herc enters holding a large trophy. He presents the trophy to Kennie and Cholly as the audience continues to applaud. The photographer approaches Tracy and shows her a photo of Ramon's ten-car masterpiece before it got buffed. THE CHORUS OF THE SONG PLAYS AS THE CAMERA pulls out of the Heavalo and up into the sky. The bombed-out buildings of the South Bronx can be seen below as the CAMERA MOVES SLOWLY SOUTH back toward Manhattan.

Hip Hop Interviews

Interview with Afrika Bambaataa
February 20th, 1982

My father and mother is from America, right? From New York. But their parents, my father's side is from Jamaica and my mother's side is from Barbados.

How old are you?
I don't give my age out. I let everybody figure that out for theirselves. Cause I feel you can communicate with all people without their knowing your age. Whether you're talking to a senior citizen or young ones. A lot of people be wanting to find out my age, but I let them think what they want to think.

What kind of work does your father do?
Hmmm. I know he's working at the hospital. I don't know as what. My mother is a nurse. My father don't live with me now. I live with my mother.

You have a big family?
No, I'm the only one. But there's a lot of people that are like family. A lot of people be coming back and forth through the house. Friends, godsisters, godbrothers.

You grew up in the Bronx?
The Southeast Bronx. Bronx River Houses. On east 174th Street.

What was it like growing up there?
This is the 1960s, '70s. In the '80s I moved uptown in the North Bronx. Sixties was nice. It's a time we was going through a lot of changes. James Brown came out with "I'm Black and I'm Proud." Everybody started having self awareness of our culture. Plus we

was into a lot of different things, like the Black Panther Party. Then the Five Percent Nation, then the Nation of Islaam.

You were involved in the Black Panthers?
They used to have a chapter on Boston Road. Used to go check out their meetings and things like that. Then when the street gangs came in, I was involved in one of the largest black street gangs in the city, The Black Spades. From there I went to the Five Percent.

What year were you involved in the Black Spades?
Umm, 1970 to 1975.

Who ran the Black Spades?
There was a lot of different leaders. They had one main leader, who was the president, then you had vice presidents, other chapter leaders, war lords, whole lot of different things whereever they had chapters. They had chapters in every precinct in the whole of New York City. Then they had chapters outside of New York State. There's a lot of history on the Black Spades.

Do they still exist?
They've broken up into different groups or crews. Like Zulu Nation. A lot of members of the Spades are in the Zulu Nation. Lot of members of the Spades are in the Casanova Crew. Lot of members of the Spades are in the Gestapo Crew. There's different groups that the Spades turned into.

What kind of stuff were the Spades doing in 1970?
Umm, some was into violence, some was into doing thing for the community. Some was into dealing with politicians and the youth service agency. Whatever. It depends on who was running what. Myself, after I left, I joined the Five Percent Nation. I was checking out their stuff when I got into Islaam. Then from the Five Percent I went into the Nation of Islaam under the Honorable Elijiah Mohhamed. kI got into that from about 1973 all the way

into the present. After his son, Wallace D, took over, that's when I left. But when it comes to, say, like you're in church and you don't go to church, that means Christians and Catholics, but you don't go to the Catholic Church every week, by nature of your family, you're a Catholic. I feel I'm still a Muslim. If they ever call for all of us to come back, for teachers or whatever, then I will go. Under Wallace D., I wasn't satisfied with what he was doing.

I'd like to get some idea of what if was like when you were growing up.
I was always into cultural things and helping out in the community in Bronx River Center. Plus I had a big leadership with a lot of youth in the neighborhood. I wsa dealing with politicians at certain times. Say like a politician needed help with signatures. I would get out into the community and try to get people to vote. If people needed meetings with youths, to find out what were their problems, I would arrange it in the Bronx River Center, where hundreds of youths would come from different areas to meeting with police, politicians or community people. Also raise money for certain groups. In 71 or 72, we raised up some money for Sickle Cell Enemia.

Were you ever into violence?
I was into street gang violence too. That's part of the whole thing of growing up in the Southeast Bronx. If you was in a gang you was doing what the gang was doing. If it was violence, it was violence. Some was good. I don't be speaking on all the stuff we be doing like that. We had our times. Other street gangs and people you don't like. I was a person who negotiated to get the gangs to stop fighting. Same with like crews they have now. When they have trouble, we try and get it all squashed, cause we don't need none of that now. It's about survival and dealing with economics, keeping our people moving on.

Could you give an example of a fight between two gangs?

I don't really be speaking on stuff that happened back then dealing with the gangs cause that's really like negative. I try to leave the negative alone and deal with the positive.

Did any of your good friends get killed in this period?
Yeah, some people got killed, stuff like that. We had articles where some people got killed by police on Pelham Parkway and a big protest and all that stuff went down. People at the Amsterdam News was involved.

When did you first get your turntables?
I been playing, we used to have regular parties where you just put on a record, take it off, if you want to call that deejaying, back in 1970. First time I seen someone with two turntables was when this brother Kool Dee came out. That was around 1975. He had a big coffin with two turntables, amps and everything. That blew a lot of people's minds seeing him playing like that. He was playing regular disco records, whatever was on the radio. He started playing and everybody at the party was doing the Bus Stop, the Bump, all that different type of dances.

Is this when the song Apache came out?
No, Apache wasn't out. It was out in 1973, since before we started deejaying. I had Apache since it came out. I wasn't a deejay at the time. But when this brother by the name of Kool Herc came out of the West Bronx, and he had this different form of music that nobody had never heard, all it was was a bunch of percussion and breaks, he just kept running it running it. Then he started saying "rock on my mellow, rock on, to the beat and you don't stop." The records he was playing, I said, wow, I got all those types of records since 1963. I got a large collection of records.

What kind of records was he playing?
He would take the best part of records, the break, and keep that going, instead of letting the words come in. Everybody would

keep dancing. Somebody might be talking over the record, or telling people what dance to do, do the Bus Stop, do the Bump. It started with Kool DJ Herc in the West Bronx. He's Jamaican. The toasting that the Jamaican's do, that's the other side of the record, dub side. They'd rap over it. He took that to American music and he started using echo and saying "rock, rock, rock." He might not mix it because he wasn't all that into mixing, but by the time the echo finished going down, you was already dancing to another record. Everybody would say, oh, wow, see how he's rockin'. You had people rapping over the record. It wasn't like rapping with rhymes, it was just like, "Rock on, to the beat y'all."

Was he saying that?
Yeah, he was. Clark Kent. That's all in 1975. There was break dancing in 1973, but that was like with the gangs, like the Good Foot. That was a form of break dancing from James Brown's "Get on the Good Foot." Guys started dancing with each other and then the girls got involved. Girls taking out other girls, girls taking out guys, all different types of break dancing.

Interview with Jay McGluery, February 26, 1982

We all grew up at that Bronx River neighborhood projects. I went to P.S. 106. During our youth, we was like any other kids. Our families wasn't well off or anything like that. Myself, I was sports inclined. I played a lot of football, a lot of basketball, but Bam wasn't the athletic type. He was more into music. Ever since I known him he was the music man. At the time he was heavily into Sly and the Family Stone. And he had every album you could name about Sly. Also, he had all kinds of rock albums. Three Dog Night, Redbone...His mother was a nurse, but she was constantly on the go. The center wasn't here, this was all grassy area. All the fellows and girls, we had no where to go. We didn't have a gym or anything for recreation, so we used to go to Bam's house. He had all the records and we used to have a clubhouse party there.

Before we knew it, the Black Spades orginated at the Bronxdale Projects. We became familiar with the people and joined the organization. And before I know it, I wind up as Warlord of this division right here at Bronx River. Bam at the time was more or less a spokesperson, or more supervisor. As far as any conflict with people, with each other, Bam would try to settle it. He would get the final say and try and straighten the fellows out.

How did he fall into that position?
Good question.

Was he trying to promote peace within the gang?
Right, beautiful. See Bam was more communications. He knows a lot of people. At the time there was a lot of gangs. We had Skulls, Reapers, Immortals. There were so many. And Bam knew all these people. He knew at least five people out of every gang.

How did he meet these guys?
All the schools are close. If you go to school, you meet this guy, and that guy. Once you get out of school you return to your clique and then you would hate this guy for some reason that was really crazy. But that's the way it was. And Bam just knew a lot of people. To make peace or make war. He was a funny guy. He never participated in sports. He was strictly a music man ever since childhood. Even when he was in the Muslims he was musically inclined. That's all this guy did is play music, music, music. I think deejays really started getting their share of publicity in 1973. That's when it really started coming on heavy. Also was this other young man named DJ Kool Herc. As we started getting older, around 16 or 17, we used to have war games. Bam, he was kind of nutty. He's the one who got all the fellas into getting bow and arrows. Not the real ones, they was practice bows and arrows. They was real points, but not hunting points. Hunting points is a blade, really dangerous. These, which you could buy in a store,

were called "target." Still, if it goes into your body you'd probably get killed.

He wanted everybody to get those?
Yes, he did start everybody. He was a leader. He was the first. We used to go over by the train tracks, right here by Bronx River, and we used to shoot the bow and arrow. We'd go down there on the train tracks. We called it hunting, and we didn't even have a hunting license. And there's rabbits down there if you get up early in the morning. None of us never hit one cause we wasn't that good. But Bam and us would go down there and a few other guys from the Spades. We'd save our Youth Core checks cause those were the jobs we had. Every year we'd work for the Youth Core in the summer. We was working with kids, assistant counselors. Bam was pretty much of a leader and he was kind of a crazy guy in his own way. Then after that, we had war games. We used to have half the project. Bam lived on the other side of the project from me, right? I lived close to the center. Bam lived on the back side. So he used to get all his friends on that side against my side. We used to fight against each other. Not real fighting, but if you happened to come along and see us, you'd swear we was really hating each other. That's the way we played. We threw bottles at each other like we was trying to kill each other. In our hearts we was playing. Bambaataa, this guy, one time he came to #135 on my side. He got some gasoline and put the gasoline all in front of the building and strikes a match, talkin' about nobody is leaving this building. So the building is burning up. The front stoop is on fire, locking everyone in. Eventually, sopme of the guys jumped out on the sides of the fire and we started chasing him all through the project. He was running. Some times we'd catch him and we'd pound on him like we'd beat him half to death. And after that we'd run and he'd get about five guys and they'd chase one of us the same way. Like I say, we was all playing.

Were there nasty wars with other gangs?

I was involved in so many. They was all nasty to tell you the truth. You might be talking about the Savage Nomads, they was located over on Southern Boulevard. And the Spades and them just did not click. If you want to look at it nationality-wise, it was blacks against Puerto Ricans. It was two pretty tough people. They had knives. We had hand guns. We made zip guns. We had a thousand zip guns and these 22-caliber bullets. Some guys were real good. They made themselves a double shot. Most were single shot. This was was pretty outrageous. You'd think it was Al Capone and Bugs Morane. Some guys would roll up to the projects in a car and shoot up everybody. The dangerous thing about that was you'd be hurting not only the people you wanted to hurt, but you'd be hitting innocent bystanders. You couldn't tell us we was wrong. We just hit everybody. They did the same thing and we did the same to them. And that thing just lasted on and on. I got out of the Spades in '75 and then I went to the Reaper's Bronx and I did about 1 and 1/2 years with them. I got out of the Spades because they was more organized in how they do things. They had a thing, what we would call a re-con unit in the Marines, like we would send four men to do a 30-man job. I got so surprised when I went to the Reapers Bronx and I seen this. Like four men equipped with hand guns and ammunition just like in the military. You get the driver and the guy riding shotgun and two guys in the back fully armed with pump shotguns and automatic pistols and the driver would have an automatic pistol. The Spades didn't believe in this. Even though they was capable of doing anything. They just had to be seen. Then wanted to show how strong they was, with a hundred men coming down the street. Chains all over them and guns sticking out of their boots. They just had to show a real strong force. They'd mob a train or mob a city bus. In fact, there was one guy named Rudy, he even stole a city bus with six other Spades. They got caught eventually and they went to jail. They did their time. I had limitations. I could only go so far. I felt like I was pretty much of a class man. I liked to do something with a little bit of style. There guys, a lot of them, just didn't care. I wasn't like that. Even though a lot of us was raised right. Our families preached to us and we didn't have no bad background. My brother's a cop, so we wasn't really raised to be that way, yet there we was.

Were you around the day the cops tried to arrest the guy walking his dog?
Oh, yes, hahaha. How could I forget? His name was Ronald Perkins. During that time they had a lot of rookie cops and the rookie cops used to wear brown uniforms. So you'd know when you see this officer in the street, he's a rookie. He's not bonafide, a veteran. So two rookie cops had a tip inside the center that the Spades were inside with guns and everything. I'm not quite sure. There was a big fight and commotion going on. This guy Perkins had a hunting dog, brown with white spots. Perkins was a mouthy type. He was also a black belt in karate. These rookie cops approached him and they was talking about something. The next thing I know, here comes a flying side-kick at the police officer. By this time one radioed in for more patrolmen, while the guy was beating up his partner. Some Spades came and took the guy's gun. By this time a hell of a lot of cops came and we was all gone. They had Mr. Perkins and his sister Rita.

They took Perkins in and worked him over?
They certainly did. He had a busted head by the time his parents got up there at the precinct. They saw the ambulance take him to Jacoby Hospital. Bam wasn't all that gung-ho with the Spades. I was once.

He wasn't into the whole violence scene?
No, not at all. He was pretty much a supervisor. You must treat the ladies with dignity.

This is about the same time the police are hunting down the Black Liberation Army?

We used to get a hell of a lot of harrassment from the police officers in the community. First of all, it was the 41st Precinct. They moved, but they was right over here in Parkchester. Most of them were white, very rascist. Most of us would be stopped and thrown against the wall. That made us stick together into gangs and stuff. And here they had a lot of white gangs, anyway. The cops harrassed us. Sometime beat us up, kick us in the groin, nasty stuff. If they wanted any cooperation from us they would never get it.

These were white cops mostly?
Matter of fact, I had seen a few black officers but they were never patrolling our neighborhood. Some of the cops was so gung-ho there was no reasoning with them. Like if you'd get stopped for a traffic violation, the cops were so nasty they might run you in. Just praying for you to come out with your face wrong and then you got a fist or a foot. Then some other cops would join in. "Oh, you giving a fellow officer a hard time, what is this?" Then they arrest you on jive charges. It was rough with these police guys. But to get back to Black Liberation, a lot of guys was young. Those guys were a little bit older than us. They used to say: You know we're the leaders for some militant organization. I remember I was young but I understood enough what he was talking about. No way in the world is he going to mistake me for those guys. We had zip guns. Those guys had damn near military gear, machine guns, 45 automatics. We didn't graduate to that stuff yet. We might have had heart like them but we didn't have our hands on any kind of equipment. Bullet proof vests, none of that stuff. Bam and I used to get harrassed a lot, especially in Junior High School. We used to show our colors. Bam went to 125. I went to 127. That's probably about 3 1/2 miles away from each other. And these areas was predominantly white areas and they didn't want no blacks in there, especially going to school. Always, until this very day it is a controversial thing there. Now we used to catch the 42 bus and there'd be a bunch of white gangs out there. They was

really gonna do some work. And the police would come and a few cops would come and tell us to keep walking. And here these guys had sticks, chains, and if that wasus, we would have been arrested on the spot. Get our face busted in. But these guys, they was standing on the street ready to take our lives. And believe they would try to take our lives. I had a few friends with busted heads and stab wounds and all that kind of crazy stuff. So the law was pretty much for those guys. So once we got away from the Junior High School was pretty much stayed away from these areas. Cause there was times when we felt threatened enough that we'd call reinforcements. Make a telephone call and we'd have about fifty guys coming up on buses. By the time they get half way, somebody had already phoned the police, who met them halfway, and they'd get arrested and we'd still be in the position where we started. So it was pretty rough. They was very racist, those guys.

What's the name of the Black Spade who got killed by the police?
Soulski. I only knew him by his nickname. By this time I was out of the Spades. He got shot in 1975. I remember when we used to go to 127 to play basketball. This must have been '74. I asked him, cause I seen him, he was 5' 7", nice build, athletic build. I saw those qualities in him, so I asked him, would you like to join the Spades? And he nodded his head, no. I saw some kind of quality in him. I liked him. He said no and I left it at that. I never thought anything of it. Before I know it, he was a Spade. Before I know it again, he was the President, Bronx River. Things were pretty good with him and Bam. He kept the same position as supervisor, but Soulski took over even more. He was kind of gung-ho. He had a lot of personality. He had feelings for people. He was attending trade school. He had some intelligence. He wasn't an A student, average student. He was a likeable guy. Everybody liked him. They knew he was in the Spades, they know the Spades are nothing but hell raisers. Most of them were like that. He was one of the good ones. He had a nice girlfriend. She was studying to be a nurse. Here was a woman who I thought would never see a man

like him. Just shows you the way the world turns. He had no other girls. He was a leader. Lot of people looked up to him. You'd think he was 6'3" or something he got that respect.

He got shot when he was 17?
Yeah, exactly.

Was he Bam's best friend?
Yes, you could say that. Matter of fact, Soulski came from a nice background. His mother and father had good city jobs and they lived in a co-op on Webster Avenue. You had to pay nice rent. Also he had some sisters and one brother. He had a nice home where he could go, bathe, shower, get three meals a day. Being that Bambatta was an only child and his mother stayed away, he was kind of spoiled too. Soulski used to spend nights over there. Being that he's the president, he was always over here. Might was well say he made his home at Bambatta's. He had his clothing there, his toothpaste, everything. So in a way he lived there for a while.

If Bam had been in that car that night he probably would have been killed.
Without a doubt. They should call the man Lucky Luciano because when it came to some real high stuff where some people would get caught at the scene, or gunned down, Bam was never there. You could call him Lucky Bam. He was never there, or he just missed it. Something came up and boom, he was elsewhere.

How long after Soulski was shot that Bam left the Spades?
There was a bunch a commotion about who done it and why.

I know in '76 Bam started the Zulu Nation.
Definitely. Okay, somewhere in late '75. Soulski was really the last of the Spades. All the old timers dropped out. Some of us had different goals in life. Some of us was getting really serious about

different women. Some went to service. Some died. Some went to college. Everything spread out. So we was growing up and Bam was still stuck with the Spades. Soulski was really the juice and battery of the Spades. He was the motivator. He would urge the men to fly their colors. Somewhere in late '75 there was me, Bambaataa, Goodrich, Desota, Pearson, Cross, Pearson. Eight guys. From that day on Bam had an idea in his head. He wanted to start giving parties. Now he graduated from being crazy guys to being businessmen. He wanted to make money. So at the time he formed a little organization. I'm trying to think of what he called it before the Zulu Nation. Bam, being that he was the deejay, everybody went to his mom's house and he's got any record you name, white, black...But Bam, he'd play hard rock. Here it is, this guy into some hard rock in this community who started all this. I'll never forget it. We all sat in the middle of the center on the benches. How can we make money? Let's throw some parties at the old center. At the time I broke away. We had pull. We'd get in the center free. We'd charge 50 cents and sell franks. It would be extremely crowded. It was okay. After a while, me and Pearson, Cross, Desota decided to split because Bam was starting to attract more of a younger crowd that we were.

What about Kool Herc?
Kool Herc wasn't on the scene with me then. I met Herc in '76. I didn't know anything until the late part of '76. Bam probably heard of him, seeing as how he ws our deejay. Dejays knew about all other deejays and what was going down with the sound. It wasn't my concern. All I knew was Bambaataa. I didn't know any other deejay. So we left Bam and started our own organization called The Players. First Bam called his The Zulus. Then later on Bam called it The Zulu Nation and it was growing.

How quickly was it growing?
I don't know. That guy's got some kind of gift with those kids. I don't believe it.

Like the Pied Piper of Rap?
Exactly. I have never in my life experienced anybody like him. He had kids from all other boroughs. Staten Island, Long Island, Amityville, Harlem, West 4th Street, Queens, Brooklyn, Manhattan.

They all wanted to be part of the mighty Zulu Nation.
Exactly. I used to see these guys by the thousands. There was so many people here when Bam gave a party. I was just so unbelievable. How in the hell this this guy get so many people? It was like he had a gift. I don't know what it is, cause he ain't a great speaker, like myself. He's average. I don't even think he knows. But there's something that man has done.

He has a moral force. He doesn't smoke, drink or use drugs.
That's true.

He's got a peaceful image.
Right, okay. I never drank. I never got high in my life. Never touched no cocaine. I never indulged in sniffing glue when we was growing up. I don't drink no beer. But still...I mean, all those kids, it was unbelievable. And he's got them trained so that if he told them to kill somebody, they'll do it. Without any hesitation. If he wanted somebody beat-up you best believe they'd be well taken care of if he abused his power. This was the early days of the Zulu Nation. These guys will do anything he says. If he says "burn the center down," they'll burn the center.

Is it still growing or has it leveled off?
Yes [still growing]. I don't know, but I'd say he's got way over a thousand members. It might run into four or five thousand. I don't know. Everywhere I go, I see them writing on the wall. What? They've been here too? I've got a niece in Queens and she was telling me about some kids talking about the Zulu Nation. He got

some kind of power. I don't know what it is, but he's got it. I must say, being that he's older was had seen a lot with drugs. We had a lot of friends die cause of drugs or shot cause of drugs. They was like our big brothers. We seen what a dope fiend looks like when he's nodding out. How embarrassing it is for the family, how shameful it is to come by and see their brother out there, so we all knew this. I guess that's why to this day Bam will preach to the kids about don't use drugs, any kind of drugs. He's against cigarettes. Try your best to stay in school, at least until you have a diploma. He does preach this. I know this for a fact. I've heard him say this many times. And if you have any kind of arguments against him, one of the main things he'll bring up, he said, "I teach them not to drink, not to smoke." He got that from the Muslims. When he starts to talk like that you can feel the vibrations from them. And stay in school. Yep.

When the Spades first got together, wasn't one of the things they wanted to do was get rid of the dope pushers?
Numero uno. This cause great problems for us because we grew up knowing these guys. I couldn't see myself beating up some guy I knew for so many years just because he was sick from this stuff. Yet, they were causing great harm because they was snatching our mother's pocketbooks in the community. So we came to the conclusion, we won't do it, we'll let them do it. We'll point them out. So we used to stand out there, he's one, he's a pusher. He'd be eliminated that night. That one. He's get a good beating that night. And you scare them. See, our main goal was to get the pushers. If you get the pushers, then you don't have to worry about the users. A user is helpless, he's sick. So you get the ones that know better. You give them a good lesson. You say, listen here, whatever you do is your business, but you ain't gonna do it on this Bronx River turf.

These guys are in their early 20's and you guys are like 14, 15.

Exactly. We was babies. We got highly respected for it. It wasn't like one guy. There would be 50 guys. Fifty young youths sticking together like that and he's gonna change his mind real quick. No matter how big, how strong you are, you ain't gonna fight 50 men. These guys used to back down. I seen these guys punch out some big guys. We cleaned up the drug problem. If we knew you was a pusher, either you got eliminated or you got badly beaten. We knew the pushers. They watched us grow up. So we'd like talk to them. We know how it is, you're sick, you gotta have your fix. but if you can, try to avoid being in the public eye. Why don't you go up on the top floor somewhere and take an OD? That's how we'd tell them. We gotta spare you cause we know you, but we have some other friends visiting us from out of town. And if they catch you like that, then they're gonna punish you. Same way if we go to some of our other guy's turf.

Did the drug problem come back after the gangs broke up?
Oh, yes. But now there's a lot of youth that don't use drugs, but they's pushers themselves. They're capable of firing automatic weapons. Most of them pushers. Now they got a lot of sophisticated drug addicts. These guys got good city jobs. They fit in society well. There's a whole bunch of them like that.

Interview with Phase 2, Summer 1983

I was born in Manhattan. I don't know what you want to hear. Basically, my mother and father are working class. Most of the writers back then were from the working class.

Did your mother and father live together?
For a time. My father worked maintenance somewhere downtown. My mother lived in Manhattan most of her life. But I grew up in the Bronx. The neighborhood is different now. My grandmother came from the West Indies over here. My father is from down South, I believe. The rest of my family is from Panama, West

Indies. That's the side of the family I most identify with. My parents tried to bring me up to know the basic difference between right and wrong. Grew up between Morrisana and Longwood. It was a hell of a lot better. Buildings were still standing. People were less hostile. Less crime in the area. Around 1965. It has changed like crazy. Like you don't even want to be there. That's how I feel. You live there, but, so what, the shit is like crazy. I don't like it there. Even in '74 the buildings were still standing. I'm talking about the early '70s. The shit started with the blackout in '77. That just totaled the whole damn neighborhood. People ransacked all the stores and the businesses never came up out of it. You had all these abandoned buildings and abandoned stores. The blackout was the start of something bad.

How old are you?
That's not important is it? 'Cause I won't tell anybody. I'd rather not tell. Nothing personal. If you said 21 in the article, someone would say he's lying.

Around '69, '70, that's when the gangs started to come back.
Yeah. I wouldn't know exactly when it happened. I definately saw it all happen in my neighborhood.

Did you join a gang?
Naw, man. I didn't see the point. It wasn't something I was threatened by. All the guys in my neighborhood, they just joined a gang if they wanted to join. Our immediate area was so different. The guys in the projects were subjected to that shit. But the guys in our area, I can't speak for Melrose, cause it was a little stronger in their area, see a half mile from us it was gangs galore, Savage Nomads, Savage Skulls, Seven Immortals, Roman Kings. It was wild. Once in a while people would come running around in my neighborhood.

What year did you start writing?

71. I wrote Phase2 because, let's put it like this. I don't know if you'll understand it, it just like somebody tagging you. They keep calling you the same name. I just got stuck on the name. Using it, you know. It's like one day we had given this party and when we were getting ready to give another party, I said, we'll call this one phase two. But the other party was not phase one. For some reason I discovered something. Like someone put a notion in my head that's supposed to be, like it was destiny, boom, and I don't know why but from that day I was stuck with the name. Like it had a meaning to me. And I don't know why but from that day I stuck with the name, like it had a meaning to me. That's what I called it, but I never considered my name Phase2, you see what I'm saying? That was always what I wrote. I write Phase2 but I'm not Phase2. People call me Phase2, but my friends don't call me Phase2. I used to get disgusted when people used to call me that because they couldn't relate to me any other way. When I was the plain old guy that I was, then everyone said, so what? But when everyone discovered I was Phase2, everybody started, hey, Phase, whattsup? I didn't care for it. I really tried to keep that image that Blade has now, before Blade had that image, low profile. I never used to tell anyone what I wrote. For quite a while nobody knew who I was. I told people that knew me, don't tell anyone I write that. That was a lot of the fun of it. You could sit around and people would say, damn you know who I want to meet? Phase2. And you're just sitting right next to them.

You saw Taki when he first went up?
Not really. I saw his name, but I think he was dying out when I seen him. I don't remember Taki getting up. I mean the guy never struck me as a martyr. He was one of the guys who first started tagging his name. Not the original guy, but one of the guys. Everybody keeps saying he was the first, but he wasn't. If I start graffiti and you pick up on it and do it better than me, so it's like, hey, I'm not necessarily insignificant. He picked up on what other guys was doing and took it to another stage. He took it to the

subways. Julio was out there writing in the streets. Taki said, hey, I'm gonna do this guy one better. I'm gonna start bombing all the train stations. That's what it was.

Taki was in Manhattan. So he was where all the press saw his work. So he got publicity.
True. Definetly. But you gotta understand this, in the Bronx, Taki was like, so what? But there are some people who was so into the shit it was crazy, and they were all over the city. I'm not gonna take anything away from Taki. He more or less started that influence to a certain extent. Guys were saying, damn, maybe I should do that. Guys that weren't writing, civilians. Those are the guys who influenced other writers. He didn necessarily, all by himself, start a movement of 4,5,6 hundred guys. Those guys were also influencing a lot of guys behind them. Somebody to say, Joe 182, not Taki 183. I think there's only one guy in the Bronx who started 30, 40 guys writing, Lee. Lee 163, the first Lee. Not putting anyone down, if your name is Lee, your name is Lee. I'm sure he started that many guys.

The gangs put their names up?
Yeah, it was all happening at the same time. I have limited knowledge on gang writing. Guys would write their names, like Kano, Black Spades, 5th Division. All that was happening around the same time. We was going stronger that that. And you even had guys in gangs writing on trains. Brooklyn was a whole different story. Brooklyn had these cliques, I don't know if they were gangs or what, they could have been out killing people, Last Survivors, Avenue Kings, and they always had these beautiful signatures next to the gang name. That's something to think about.

There's a difference between writing in a gang and writing solo?
Do you see a difference? I can relate to what you're saying. Basically it was the same thing. For people to know you existed. If anything, through identifying with names, it was the repetition.

Like you might see 5th Division 750 times, 2nd Division 4 times. Sometimes it was a turf thing. You come in there and you're from the Skulls, you say, shit, this is Spade turf. Especially when you saw it big, then you knew if was turf. At times, guys would do it to slander other guys. The closer you got to another gang's territory, like we're bad, check this out. In a sense, it's the same thing happening with the writers, but as a less hostile thing. We came into your neighborhood.

You got a lot of respect from the gangs because you were up everywhere?
I don't know. A lot of guys in gangs were relating to this. You had guys in gangs who were also writing on trains and everyone was like a family. I think when you wrote on trains, it's always a family. For the guys that are really into it. They stick together. There's none of that style wars shit. Even these guys still have respect for each other because you know there's a limit to how much respect you have give to the other 70% that's out there. The mentality is totally different. It's all about society. It's a social change. I wasn't running around starving without a dime in my pocket. I didn't have the best shit, there were guys who had more, guys who had less, but none of us was at the point wehre, damn I can't even get a dollar. Lot of these guys out here, first of all they're never satisfied, they're always taking shit from each other. The reason why you see graffiti made with two different pictures is because the social change out here. There's always been two basic types. People write for different reasons, but either you're in or you're out. The guys that are dedicated and the guys that just do it. I think dedication is at different levels. This is something that still holds meaning for you. It holds strength. It's not some bullshit that's not solid. Boom. I'm out here because I want to be a bomber, man. I want to get up and I want everybody to see it. Not because, I'm gonna bomb, man, there's nothing else to do, fuck it, so it's not like you don't give a shit. Either you're devoted or you're just out there bullshitting and you don't know what you're

doing. When you say two different types of writers, either you're down or you're not down. Then you got those guys in between. You got guys out there writing everyday, but their ignorance still has them crossing out other people's names. Maybe because of their youth. Age is a bugged-out thing. When you were 15 or 16, these guys are still thinking out of synch. We would think of ingenious ways to do negative things. So that they never really looked as negative as they were. If you put an X over somebody's name, boom, it's there and you know it. If we didn't want a guy on the line who was going around fucking with other people's pieces, we'd just paint right over him. Not cross it out, paint right over it. How long is that guy gonna last? He's got to give in or get out. If you cross out, then I just do it back to you. But if you got 20 guys going over your pieces, and you do understand that respect, now that might not even work cause of the mentality. That's what kept the unity going on for so long. Even if guys quit, four years later they'd say, yeah, I remember when we used to ride the trains. And that to me is some kind of devotion. The guys that are really into graffiti, another ten years from now, they'll still be saying, yeah, I remember when we used to ride the trains. That's the guys I respect more than anyone else. You gotta respect writers. I feel like this, I'm somewhat of an authority. I helped create this. I know what the bullshit is. I know what's garbage and what isn't. I'm looking at it, I know. I know these guys can paint, but yet other guys will not acknowledge it. There was always that respect where you'd say, I can't stand him, I hate his guts, man, he's a sucker, but he damn sure can paint. It's back to society and environment and that family thing. If you take these guys who have a more positive attitude and a more negative attitude, and check out their backgrounds. I think now you got more white kids writing on trains than before. But see that's new, that "fucking white boy." You rode on trains, hey, whatsup? In a sense you could relate to them, you could hang out together. It wasn't like I lived in the South Bronx and I didn't know anything but blacks and ricans. I went to school, mostly white kids. This was P.S. 86

on 195th St. And nowadays, if you would try to do that shit to me, I'd say, you're crazy. I'm not going up in that white neighborhood. Social change. Like I said, back then, everything was everything. My mother always told me, you're going to good schools. I always knew I was going to good schools. I could go to school with all these different kids.

You started writing in 72? With just magic markers?
Markers and paint. The markers were first, but I wasn't doing it then. When we first started it was markers and spray paint. Basically, I think it was on stations. I don't know. I don't even know. I don't even know who started hitting the insides of trains first. I know it was those guys on Broadway. Broadway writers hit the insides. Who started it with paint? Supposedly a guy named RA184. This is quoted from Joe 182. Supposedly a guy named Russell Aronson. I was told that Joe said it himself. So that's something to think about.

Did you know Stay High?
Yeah. Nobody hung out with Stay High, except his partner. We knew him good and it was always good to see the guy. Stay High was basically by himself.

Stay High and Super Kool, were they important people?
Definitely. All these guys now don't realize that we went through a whole stage they didn't even have to go through. It was like I wrote the book, here it is, learn it. We didn't have that. We went from one stage to the next at random. You did something, got an idea and threw it up on the train. Then everybody else said, hmmm, picked up on it.

When did you first get the idea for the bubble letters?
I believe in 1973.

Let's talk about your specific contributions.

Well, in 1973 all the pieces started. In 1973 Super Kool came out with his shit. I can't say people doing giant signatures influenced other guys to do masterpieces. All I know is that Super Kool started writing his signature...and actually filling it in. That was the first guy to take the time to fill in an outline and come up with something bigger on the trains. At the time, the damn thing wouldn't be any bigger than this bottle. Super Kool introduced the masterpiece 'cause no one else wanted to do it 'cause it was taking up too much spray paint. Everybody said, no, man, I'm not doing it 'cause that's a whole can of paint.

Before then, the outsides of trains just had tags?
Just regular tags. The only thing bigger at the time was...in train stations. The Bronx had awakened. Bronx and Manhattan were on the same level as far as everyone bombing. Bronx and Manhattan were already bombed out. Then what revolutionized the whole thing is when this guy Super Kool came out with this piece. Everybody was damn negative about it. Even I said, yeah, that shit is crazy. 'Cause with one can of paint you could write your name so many damn times. But then everybody picked up on it. I made up letters that looked like my signature. I bubbled them. I did not make my signature bigger. I drew those same letters with depth. I must have had about 60 different signature changes. I changed the "2" 'cause other people were using my "II." The gap between the "p" and the "h" really fucked with me. The "p" tended to drift away from the other letters. I don't remember if it was a mistake or on purpose that the "h" and the "p" began fusing together. Most of the names related to a nickname. After Phase came out, you'd see tags like Dream, Think. I think "phase" opened the way for different kinds of names.

Who inspired you to bomb?
Cay 161. I think he was one of the earliest guys that really destroyed trains.

When was he hitting?
In 1972.

How big was your family?
Not that big. Couple sisters and a brother. I'm the youngest.

How did your family feel about it?
My mother thought, this shit is crazy, writing on trains. At first. But she was glad something good came out of it. In 1982 she didn't want to hear that shit. Anything but graffiti, please. I've had enough of that. I don't even know who she found out about my writing on trains.

How about your brother?
I don't want to get into all that shit. I'm not going to get into detail. Sweet Duke was my only brother. Me and him would go writing all the time. Eventually my mother found out I was writing. I guess I was hitting on things too. She used to see that shit all the time. I had shit on paper. When my friends would come into the building, they'd write all over the halls. She knew they were coming up there doing that shit. At first she didn't dig it at all. Then she accepted it to a certain degree. Lee was crazy at first. Then he quit. I was the mad man that became obsessed with the shit.

Were you considered a master in 1972?
Not in my eyes. I started killing the lines after Super Kool. At one time, guys were bombing the lines so heavy that you couldn't do shit. I was writing with Lee a lot. At that time, Lee was the king of the 2's, 4's and 5's. He was riding the trains and hitting them with marker and paint. Everybody saw his name. We had nothing else to do, so we went hitting.

What sort of reputation did Stay High have?

Phantom. Not too many people knew him.

How about his style?
His tag was something. That's why everyone got hip to him. A lot of people got up more than Stay High. But he got around. Dice198 was destroying the line. Hondo. But Stay High had that name.

Was Stay High considered an innovator, like Super Kool?
With the stick figure. When Super Kool started writing everybody started writing "super" something. Stay Swift, Stay Kool, I'm Bad. It started something.

Interview with Kool Herc, March 2, 1982

Were you born in Jamaica?
Yes, Kingston. I came to New York in 1967, when I was 12 years old.

Were you familiar with toasting at 12?
Not really. I was familiar with the island music.

When did you get the name Kool Herc?
That came from school and both parts linked from different places. The neighborhood wanted nicknames and I be cool. At school I was an athlete, and one guy started calling me Hercules. It was a nickname he tried to stick on me, but I didn't like it. I resented it. Then I thought about it and broke it down and came up with Herc. That sounds rare, and that was it. Kept everybody happy, kept me happy.

When did you name your speakers the Herculords?
I was trying to make the people see what their money was being spent on. On music and equipment. We had some Shure columns.

Did you have a mike and echo?

Yeah, I always had the mike and echo-chamber.

I'm really interested in the development of rap music and I'd like to know when you started using the mike?
I always did. I never liked to disturb the record. I always knew my records and I knew when it was going to pause, for me to throw in one of two words. Mainly the rap came up at school where a certain joke would come up, or a certain saying. I just started to broadcast it. Anything they like. It's the joint, meaning the music is good. When we say that it means the record is good. When we say joint after joint, it means we're having a barrage of good music. We watch the flow of the party, how everybody is moving. The rythm gets you and if you come up with a word that fits in overnight, you go home and the next couple days you hear them saying it around.

You had a couple of deejays with you?
Clark Kent. The first was Coke-La-Rock. He was an emcee. We spoke about what was happening around us. We never fantasized. When we say something we identify ourselves as "no pushovers." It was a balance of communication with them. We let them know they're the ones putting us on and we're gonna put them on as we go up. We're not just getting stardom. We're not suckers. We never based our music on cuts. We just played good music. Just bring the music in, the music speaks for itself.

Bambaataa told me he heard about you in late 1974? And at the time his crowd was into Kool Dee.
Me and Bam got together just naturally. Kool Dee hop on the whole phase when it broke out. The equipment I'm trying to get now? His mother went out at one time and bought it. He got into it because it was something coming up. He had no experience. Then after that Bambaataa came up. Somebody hired me to come over. I met Bam and we started talking. He said come to my house to see his records. I told him I couldn't do it. I went on and met the

people. I got to know a few people out at Bronx River and I started to hang out there. Then one summer I was bicycle riding and I heard some music playing. I rode around back and I looked up and I saw Bam. I said, oh, wow, I never knew he picked up on playing music. Then I started hearing music I never heard before. I was waiting for that. 'Cause every time I play something I hear it everywhere I go. I didn't like stuff like that. I was always trying to search and find new stuff and when I do find it, I give the person recognition. I don't bite people's stuff. But nobody never approached me, never talked to me about getting into it. They just jump in and picked it up. Not one until this day say, Herc, how do you go about it? I want to do what you're doing. I like what you're doing. I was willing. But I don't open myself up because they say, wow, he's looking for friends. I started going to Bam's parties because I was guaranteed to hear music that I never heard before. Until this day, he's the only deejay I really respect. Bam is an ally as far as who I trade music with. Deejays don't like to go to other deejays and ask them what the record is. But with me and Bam, that's open. We're on the search. I could please Bam at a party knowing that he's in the house, and I play a lot of the records that he gave recognition too. And he'd do the same for me. If I go to a party as ask them to play a reggae record, they won't play it. I don't even have to ask Bam. He'll probably see me there and start playing it. That's communication, friendship.

What's the difference between rap in New York and Jamaica?
It wasn't supposed to take a Jamaican form. A lot of people don't know I'm from Jamaica. You have to be born there to understand certain words they use.

Is "that's the joint?" Jamaican?
No. It's just the slang from that time of year. As the year go on, you find new words. Or a fan will come up and tell you, this is good and tip you. I have a lot of tips. I please the person that tell me something when I see them. Me and them communicating.

Bam told me that between 1975 and '76, only three deejays were doing the style, Bam, Flash and you.
Naw, that Flash, he came in and disturbed the style. Not to the people, but in a deejay point-of-view. He started the quick cutting. My style of music, anybody could relate to. Adult and teenager could party to it. A lot of people don't like the jigga, jugga stuff because it throws you off beat. It's a lot of work if that's the style you got. But I don't have that and I don't like it. I could do it, but if I do it, my people look at me and go, hey, you're trying to be like Flash. They tell me, Herc, you be yourself. But he really turned on a lot of kids to do it and they don't recognize good disco music. I'll always play disco. What Flash did is everybody started hunting for breaks and all of a sudden the disco faded out.

You were playing breaks.
Breaks is part of the whole show.

Who started "Apache?"
I was the first. Once they hear that, they know they're going to hear Scorpio, Funky Music, and a couple of other. Once that's over, I play the slow music because you can't hype it up any more. So you bring on the slow and after that play the mellow music. Once that finish, it's the whole cycle again.

Apache came out in 1973?
No, Apache came out in 1975, '76. We had the record laying around for a long time. But one night was just stumbled into it. I bring back a lot of records.

What do you think about the Zulu Nation?
Bam is not to be blamed for them. They start trouble. It's always conflict. We do things as deejays to attract people. We say, me and Bam are going to have a battle and that's a gimmick. But the Zulus take it to heart. They'll start pulling plugs. If they decide I'll

only have an hour playing time, they cut it off. Now Bam ain't that type of person, but the people don't really back him like they should. I told Bam, I like the organization you have, give the people some membership cards. They come down, one guy stands by the door, he okays ten people. Then he'd leave and another would okay another bunch. And before you know it, there's fifty people in there. And that's not business. I'm for business. Friendship ceases when you're playing. It's very hazardous, man. When you got that many people coming in, it's hard for a man to make money. It's bad for the clientele. That's always been my conversation with him. He gets blamed a lot for what the Zulus do. Bam can't go back to a lot of places because trouble start and now the doors are closed. Bam has a lot of respect. He had to get in there and break it up. Like sometimes I have to do. Sometimes they think about it before I get there, and they take it outside. But I got hit by a crazy kid. But I'm not going to leave them alone because they're the ones that discovered me and I'm the only guy at this age that knows what they want. I lost out on my age bracket. I'm always older than the ones coming up.

It seems only the young are into rap.
Yes. Not even myself. I don't like the rap scene. I was never too much of a rapper. I could pick up rapping but at my own pace. They know I'm into disco. When I play something I know is going to be a hit, I tell my crowd. When it gets on the radio, I stop playing it.

So you don't have any plans for an emcee group?
I don't know. Flash, Melle Mel, they came to me. When I'm playing, I'm running my business. But they claim that they came to me and I didn't want to speak with them.

You don't get along with Flash?
No, we get along. We never did speak. I get and give respect. I heard about him and anybody who touch the wax is a friend in my

heart. Anybody who pick up the wax, it make me feel good. He used to come to my parties. People say, "it's Flash," but I'm not the one to walk to him. He got to come to me. Sometimes you got to do things the right and proper way. Pete DJ Jones heard about me coming up out of the Bronx and we hooked up for a battle. He came up with Starski and Flash was on his side, telling him what record to play. Pete never knew about my style. And Pete, like a fool, played my records to beat me. There was nothing he played that people hadn't heard before and know that I'd played it. Come to my backyard and do that. That battle take place at the Executive Playhouse on Jerome Avenue in early 1976. But at the time I didn't know how powerful I was and I got stabbed. I was playing at the same club. Some little discrepancy broke out and I was walking and a stranger thought I was messing with his friend. I got knifed three times. I didn't blame nobody. I could have. I could have gone on a rampage. But, hey, people here and the host gets stabbed? How you think they feel about coming to the party? After that, the door was open for Flash. I didn't find no good place. The place burnt down. Poppa couldn't find no good ranch so the herd scattered. Coke proved if you could become a deejay, you could become an emcee. Flash is in the background. Mel is the one who changed everything. Out of due respect, Flash did up his style and tricks. I got a kid who's as bad as Flash, Whiz Kid, but he came along too late.

I'm a writer, journalist, filmmaker, event producer and counterculture and cannabis activist. I started out writing black comedy, but I'm best known as the first reporter to document hip hop and the instigator of the film *Beat Street*. I also founded the Cannabis Cup, organized the first 420 ceremonies outside of Marin County, while launching the hemp movement with Jack Herer and writing some landmark conspiracy articles.

Some of my other books you might enjoy:

Why was Lincoln left unguarded when the War Department knew there were serious plots afoot against him? Why was Booth killed even though he was discovered locked inside a tobacco barn and surrounded by 25 soldiers? Why were two innocents swiftly hanged by a military tribunal and not allowed to even testify in their own defense? Find all the answers in this explosive book.

The JFK assassination was handled through CIA counterintelligence. William Harvey recruited some exiled Cubans and Johnny Roselli to kill Fidel Castro, but when JFK tried to stop violence against Cuba, that crew was diverted to kill Kennedy.

Does cannabis cure cancer? Cancer is a big subject and easily misunderstood. But there is no doubt cannabis has anti-cancer effects, so why does the US government pretend it has no legitimate medical uses?

In the 1980s the art world turned upside down as punks and graffiti artists suddenly catapulted to center stage. This insightful book captures the social environment that launched artists like Jean-Michel Basquiat, Keith Haring and Kenny Scharf, while chronicling the rise and fall of the East Village scene.

Printed in Great Britain
by Amazon